A 31-Day Devotional for Women

Read
&
Pray
& then Obey

Lindsay Roberts

RICHARD ⊕
ROBERTS
ORAL ROBERTS MINISTRIES

Copyright © 2013
Lindsay Roberts
Tulsa, Oklahoma

Published by Oral Roberts Evangelistic Association
P.O. Box 2187
Tulsa, OK 74102

BK2475

ISBN 978-0-9827018-2-9

TABLE of CONTENTS

Day 1 — Finding Life

Read Those who discover these words live, really live; body and soul, they're bursting with health (Proverbs 4:22 MSG).

This scripture says that the Word of God is life to those who find it, and health to all their flesh. But first, we have to *find* it. We aren't just automatically full of the Word of God. Thankfully, the Bible gives us a formula for how to find God's Word and the life and health that comes with it. You see, this indicates that God has a plan laid out for us. Just before that, in verses 20 and 21, the Scripture says, *My son, give attention to my words; incline your ear to my sayings. Do not let them depart from your eyes; keep them in the midst of your heart* (NKJV). That's the key.

"We aren't just automatically full of the Word of God."

To me, the Word of God is the most powerful force on the face of the earth, because with His Word, He formed and fashioned this earth. When we go into agreement with His Word, I believe we can fulfill the purpose that we are called to do in Him. When our words line up with His Word, things can change according to His plan, His purpose, and His will for our lives.

God's Word is designed and ordained to be life to those who find it. So if you want life, wouldn't it make sense to find His Word? The Bible says His Word is health to all your flesh. So if you are looking for a spiritual answer to health, wouldn't it make sense to find His Word? Satan may have a plan to hurt you, steal from you, or make you sick, according to John 10:10 NIV, which says, *The thief comes only to steal and kill and destroy,* but according to Proverbs 4:22, Father God has designed His Word to be life and health for those who are willing to get into His Word—really finding the Word, releasing faith, and acting on His will. It is all part of our ability to choose. And as Joshua 24:15 says, we are to choose this day who we will serve.

Pray Consider praying this prayer…

Father God, I thank You that the Bible says that Jesus was the Word clothed in flesh. As we find Jesus, we can find Your Word and Your will. When we can find Your Word and Your will, we can find Jesus. Thank You that Psalm 107:20 says that You sent Your Word to heal us and to deliver us from destruction. Thank You for sending Jesus as our deliverer. As we put our faith in You, we ask You to bless us according to Ephesians 3:20, which says, **…exceedingly abundantly above all that we could ask or think.** *In Jesus' name, amen.*

Obey Consider this…

I encourage you to find God's Word (the Bible). As you read it, study it, meditate on it, and make it alive in your heart, I pray that you begin to expect God to honor His Word in your life. I also encourage you to begin to meditate on Psalm 19:14, which says, *Let the words of my mouth and the meditation of my heart be acceptable in Your sight, O Lord, my strength and my Redeemer.* Allow your words to match His Words, and then begin to expect that God can turn things around for good in your life.

Day 2 The Lord's Prayer

Read And when you pray, do not use vain repetitions as the heathen do. For they think that they will be heard for their many words. Therefore do not be like them. For your Father knows the things you have need of before you ask Him. In this manner, therefore, pray: Our Father in heaven, hallowed be Your name. Your kingdom come. Your will be done on earth as it is in heaven. Give us this day our daily bread. And forgive us our debts, as we forgive our debtors. And do not lead us into temptation, but deliver us from the evil one. For Yours is the kingdom and the power and the glory forever. Amen (Matthew 6:7–13).

I believe Jesus gave us an amazing gift in the Lord's Prayer. He gave us a roadmap to a simple way we can pray, so that the necessary elements that involve living life here on Earth can be found in this concise prayer. In his Bible commentary, my father-in-law, Oral Roberts, breaks Matthew 6 down so beautifully. He helps us understand how we can apply each element to our lives today. So, let's look at Oral's thoughts and insights on this most powerful prayer.

"I believe Jesus gave us an amazing gift in the Lord's Prayer."

Our Father… The term Father signifies closeness—a close, personal relationship with our Father God, which we have through our faith in the finished work of Jesus Christ on the cross.

Which art… God exists. He is "I AM." Jesus said that when we pray, we should pray to someone who IS—someone who is alive today and who never changes. The weather changes, people change, circumstances change, but God is the same, yesterday, today and forever (Hebrews 13:8).

In heaven… Remember that God, who desires to be our Father and our Source, is in heaven. And in heaven, there is no shortage. That's why He can supply all our needs according to His riches in glory (Philippians 4:19).

Hallowed be thy name… Hallowed means holy. Jesus had reverence for the name of God. He knew that His Father was the Source of His life, so He gave Him great love, honor, and praise.

Thy kingdom come… Jesus was concerned about the earthly place we live in, but He was even more concerned about God's heavenly kingdom. Jesus taught us to pray concerning living in God and His power on earth, just as He intended when He brought God's kingdom principles to earth. So, He taught us to pray and live our daily lives expecting God's kingdom to be a part of our lives as we act on God's Word in faith, expecting miracles in every area of our lives on this earth.

Thy will be done in earth, as it is in heaven… The will of God starts in heaven, but it must be lived out in our daily lives here on earth. That's what my mother-in-law, Evelyn Roberts, called the "everydayness" of life. She truly believed God would meet our every need in a very practical, tangible way—every day. And this verse tells us that His will for our lives is to be accomplished on earth, just as it is in heaven.

Give us this day our daily bread… Jesus is talking about God's daily sustenance. In Matthew 15:25–27, He called healing the children's bread. In John 6:35, Jesus calls Himself the Bread of Life. Here, it reads that we can get daily sustenance in life through a relationship with Jesus. This includes both the things that can meet our physical needs as well as the things that can feed us spiritually.

Forgive us our trespasses as we forgive those who trespass against us... When we are trespassers or sinners against God and against people, God can offer us full and free forgiveness as we truly repent. And, in turn, we can extend our forgiveness through Christ, to others who may do us wrong as God generously gave us His very best—His Son, Jesus—to bring about our forgiveness. This doesn't mean we agree with their actions or condone them. It simply means we forgive them according to the Bible. This may or may not release them to repent and get right with God. But it releases us, spiritually speaking, from any bondage or hold the wrong done to us may try to have over us. As we forgive, it's like spiritually taking the offense out of our hands and putting it into God's hands. As we have freely received forgiveness, this indicates that we are to freely give forgiveness (Matthew 10:8).

Lead us not into temptation, but deliver us from evil... This prayer asks, "God, don't let me be left to myself when the going gets rough. Let me be in Your path when I face situations that are bigger than I am." His help can be available to us throughout our daily lives, and as we acknowledge that we need Him and ask Him for His assistance, I believe He is right there to help. And as John 6:37 says, those who come to Him in faith, He doesn't cast aside.

"...those who come to Him in faith, He doesn't cast aside."

For thine is the kingdom, and the power, and the glory, forever. Amen... God's kingdom (His Word, His will, and His ways of doing and being, according to Matthew 6:33) can triumph over all the attacks of the devil as we, in faith, call upon the name of the Lord.

Pray Consider praying this prayer...

Heavenly Father, we ask You to help us make prayer a daily part of our lives, and we thank You for teaching us this simple prayer. Thank You for giving us an instruction manual for how we can be more like You in every way. We pray that Your precious Holy Spirit would reveal to us the areas where we need help, where we can change, and where we can be better followers of Christ. In Jesus' name, amen.

Obey Consider this...

I encourage you to commit the Lord's Prayer to your memory and begin to pray it out loud on a regular basis. As you say it aloud, I believe you can begin to see how it applies to different areas of your life, and you can talk to God more specifically about the issues that concern you personally. I set my faith with you in Jesus' name, believing that you can begin to grow more and more in the areas that Jesus brings to your attention in the Lord's Prayer.

I am the bread of life. He who comes to me will never go hungry, and he who believes in me will never be thirsty.

—John 6:35 NIV

Day 3 — Spiritually Release the Hurts of the Past

Read *Remember ye not the former things, neither consider the things of old. Behold, I will do a new thing; now it shall spring forth; shall ye not know it? I will even make a way in the wilderness, and rivers in the desert* (Isaiah 43:18–19 KJV).

Is there something from your past that you never seem able to put behind you? I believe God wants us to be free from grudges, hurt feelings, guilt, unforgiveness, and fear—things that are hurts of the past. I believe there is freedom from hurts, disappointments, and pain. And I believe that God has a bright future ahead of us when we begin to "spiritually bury those bones of the past!"

" I believe there is freedom from hurts, disappointments, and pain."

Sometimes our past may have involved something extremely difficult or painful, and holding on to it may hinder chances we have of the bright future God has planned for us. Or if the past was good, we might say, "My life used to be so wonderful, and now it's just rotten." If we're living in the old glory days, it, too, can hinder growing further into our future.

Isaiah 43:18–19 KJV says, *Remember ye not the former things, neither consider the things of old. Behold, I will do a new thing; now it shall spring forth; shall ye not know it? I will even make a way in the wilderness, and rivers in the desert.* When Isaiah was inspired to write that verse,

God must have known we would be tempted to hang on to the part of the past that could hinder us. But He tells us, "Forget it and let it go." Because God did include it, it leads me to believe that He must have thought it was very important to learn to let go of hindering things from the past and the hurt that goes with them.

The faithful love of the Lord never ends! His mercies never cease. Great is his faithfulness; his mercies begin afresh each morning.

—Lamentations 3:22-23 NLT

For me, I was holding on to the pain of not being able to have children. My father had died of leukemia when I was twelve, and a few years later I found myself experiencing one crazy symptom after another. It was frightening. Finally, after a long time of doctor visits and medical tests, I was told, at the age of 18, that I would not be able to have children because of the disorder in my body.

Six years later I married Richard, and after a long struggle of trying to get pregnant, I was beginning to face the harsh reality that the possibility of having children was slowly slipping from my life. After two miscarriages, a son dying in my arms, and several surgeries, including a surgery for a hysterectomy (during which I had a miracle that made the surgery unnecessary after all), I was riding a total emotional rollercoaster. By strategically avoiding baby stores, the baby food aisles, baby showers and anything that had to do with pregnant women, I carefully avoided the subject of childbirth. But I was not healed in my body or my soul.

However, one day the Lord prompted me to sow seed by giving baby showers for some of my pregnant friends. While I felt this request from the Lord was unfair, I also realized that something had to change. So in my obedience to God's word to me, I began hosting baby showers and buying baby gifts. I spent the vast majority of these parties in the bathroom crying my guts out, but I still counted it as my seed to the Lord. No matter the struggle, attack, and pain I was enduring, I knew I had my seeds of faith in the ground. I believe that as a result of that seed and my obedience to God, I experienced a miracle that resulted in the birth of three beautiful, healthy daughters. And as they say, the rest is history! For me, I had to release the pain and devastation of my past before restoration could come.

"For me, I had to release the pain and devastation of my past before restoration could come."

Now, you may be going on like I was—emotionally digging up old hurts from your past. But when it's all over, is it ultimately worth it? Perhaps it's time to release the guilt, the shame, and the torment and the hurt of the past. You can receive God's precious healing and His mercies, which are new every morning (Lamentations 3:22–23). I encourage you to consider making a decision to put the past in the past and move forward into God's new things and allow Him to give you a bright and beautiful future according to His Word.

Pray Consider praying this prayer…

Lord, right now in the name of Jesus, I spiritually release all the hurt, bad memories, problems, and circumstances of my past that are hindering my future. I receive Your healing for these wounds, and if I have caused pain, I repent and receive Your forgiveness according to 1 John 1:9, which promises to cleanse me when I ask for Your forgiveness. By faith, the past is behind me now. Today, I am making a fresh start. Lord, thank You for setting me free so that I can have a bright new future in You, in the name of Jesus. Amen.

Obey Consider this…

Now that you have experienced the *read* and *pray* portion of today's devotional, I encourage you to walk out your healing. Dwell on the scripture that says, *Therefore if the Son makes you free, you shall be free indeed* (John 8:36), and declare your freedom throughout the day.

Therefore if the Son makes you free, you shall be free indeed.

—John 8:36

Building Faith for Your Healing

Read *The prayer of faith will save the sick, and the Lord will raise him up* (James 5:15).

"Your crawling days are over!" That is what my husband, Richard, said to Abdul, a precious man who had just been miraculously healed by God in a miracle service in the Polo Field in the great city of Jos, Nigeria. Richard conducted a healing crusade there, and Abdul's healing was one of the greatest highlights. Abdul was widely known throughout the town, and he could be seen most days begging in front of the town's post office. From what we later were told, he had never been able to walk, and people in the town knew it.

"The people were so astonished that the local media put the story in the newspapers."

What a glorious healing we witnessed that night! Abdul, "the beggar of Jos" as he was called, jumped and shouted that night on the crusade platform. The people were so astonished that the local media put the story in the newspapers.

I believe God's healing power is available to every generation that is willing to reach out to Him in faith. My father-in-law, Oral, often told the story of a little boy by the name of Willie, who had a crippling bone disease that caused one leg to be two-and-a-half inches shorter than the other. This little boy and his mother were determined to get to the Oral Roberts crusade because they had their faith set on a miracle. Nothing was going to stop them, not even the overflowing crowds.

On the final day of the crusade, little Willie and his mother could not get in the building, so his mother sent Willie in alone where he could wait in a back room near the door. When the crusade was over, as Oral was exiting the building, he passed by the room where little Willie was sitting alone. Oral stopped and asked Willie, "What are you doing here?"

So then faith comes by hearing, and hearing by the word of God.

–Romans 10:17

Willie said, "I'm waiting for Oral Roberts to pray for me to be healed."

Oral answered, "I'm Oral Roberts, and the meeting is over. I've prayed for a lot of people today, and I'm tired. But if you'll believe God with me, I'll pray for you." Willie agreed, and Oral prayed for him and left the building.

The next day, Willie and his mother shared the news of Willie's healing. He was wearing new shoes, normal shoes without a built-up heel. He was totally healed!

To see miracle healings up close and personal can be life-changing. There's just nothing like it. Richard and I have been privileged to travel all over the world and preach and pray for the sick, and we have seen countless miracles.

The Bible tells us in James 5:15, *The prayer of faith will save the sick, and the Lord will raise him up.* That word *save* means to rescue from destruction and preserve one who is in danger, to make well, and to restore to health. And the word *sick* includes the weak, feeble, powerless, and diseased. Notice that this verse is talking about more than just physical healing. This verse says that the prayer of faith can rescue us from destruction.

"…you can be healed, cured, made whole, freed from errors and sins, and able to enjoy all the aspects of God's salvation."

James 5:16 goes on to say, *Confess your trespasses to one another, and pray for one another, that you may be healed. The effective, fervent prayer of a righteous man avails much.* The word *healed* in this verse means so much more than merely healing from only physical sickness and disease. It includes the idea that you can be healed, cured, made whole, freed from errors and sins, and able to enjoy all the aspects of God's salvation. That is a very far-reaching definition of healing. And that is a good thing! Praise God, we can call on Jesus as our Savior and deliverer, and He can be there with us in our time of need as we call out to Him for His help.

Pray Consider praying this prayer…
Heavenly Father, we pray right now in the name of Jesus that whatever may be coming against us, God's miracle-working power would meet us at the point of our need.

According to the Bible, we rebuke the devil and command him to take his hands off of us. And we pray that, just like little Willie, we are being empowered by the Holy Spirit in us to stand up with boldness and determination, and believe God that this is our time for a miracle. In Jesus' name, amen.

Obey Consider this...

Now, I encourage you to take some time to read and study out some of the healing scriptures in the Bible. Write them down on paper or note cards and keep them readily available to you. You may want to speak those healing scriptures to yourself. The Bible says that faith comes by hearing and hearing by the Word of God (Romans 10:17), so I encourage you to continually hear yourself confess the Word of God and begin to expect that your own miracles can be on the way, in Jesus' name!

The effective, fervent prayer of a righteous man avails much.

–James 5:16

Day 5 Be Kind to One Another

Read *And be ye kind one to another, tenderhearted, forgiving one another, even as God for Christ's sake hath forgiven you* (Ephesians 4:32 KJV).

When my daughters were little, I used an acronym to help them remember this important principle: BYKOTA, which stands for *Be Ye Kind One To Another*. It served as a good reminder for us all, and I believe it still does today!

Kindness is defined as "the act or the state of being kind, being marked by good and charitable behavior, pleasant disposition, and concern for others." As an example of someone who modeled kind behavior throughout her life, Mother Teresa once said, "Kind words can be short and easy to speak, but their echoes are truly endless."

"But the kindness of our Father God to us can be even more effective than human goodness. His divine kindness can have the power to change things in an eternal way."

The kindness we show others can have a big impact, especially if it is genuinely undeserved. But the kindness of our Father God to us can be even more effective than human goodness. His divine kindness can have the power to change things in an eternal way.

As Romans 2:4 NIV says, *"God's kindness leads you toward repentance."* My husband, Richard, had an experience that demonstrates this principle in such a tangible way. He was backstage at a television taping, waiting with the other guests when he noticed that among the other guests was an individual who had once wronged Richard and hurt him deeply. When he saw the individual, the Holy Spirit moved on him. Richard was overwhelmed with compassion—the supernatural kindness of God that leads Him to move toward us and help us. Richard went over, hugged the individual, and apologized for holding unforgiveness in his heart about what had been done to him.

God's kindness is intended to lead you to repent...

—Romans 2:4 AMP

The moment Richard showed kindness, the person's heart immediately softened, and he repented for what he had done. He told Richard over and over that he knew what he had said and done was wrong and he was deeply sorry for all the trouble he had caused. Because of that, the Lord was able to mend the relationship, and my husband and this gentleman remained friends until the man went home to be with the Lord.

If Richard had not responded with the kindness and compassion of Jesus, I don't know what may have happened, but it seems unlikely that there would have been a restoration in the relationship that day. In this situation, it was kindness that made all the difference. Kindness allowed the Holy Spirit to come into the situation and bring healing.

Sometimes it can be difficult to be kind to others, especially if we are going through a challenge in our lives or if the other person is being hurtful and unkind to us. Such cases can seem to be some of the hardest times of all to be compassionate. But I want to encourage you to let God work in your heart and in the situation. Through the work of our Savior, Jesus Christ, on the cross, God offers us forgiveness—even when we don't deserve it. And we can choose to extend God's forgiveness, kindness, and mercy even when we may not feel like doing it. When we are willing to do that, God can do miraculous things for us in the situation that He might not be able to otherwise do.

Pray Consider praying this prayer…
Father God, I thank You for each one who is reading this today. I thank You for their lives, their gifts and talents, their families, and what the future holds for them. Lord, we thank You for Your extraordinary kindness to us, Your children. Even when we don't deserve it, You show us Your tender loving-kindness. Lord, as we receive mercy and kindness from You, help us to commit to doing our very best to share Your kindness and mercy with those around us. In Jesus' name, amen.

Obey Consider this...

An anxious heart weighs a man down, but a kind word cheers him up (Proverbs 12:25 NIV). It is my prayer that God gives us the opportunity to practice true, godly kindness today. It may seem like a very small thing to simply speak a kind, gentle, loving word to someone. But God's kindness can have a more far-reaching effect than we may realize. I believe it has the potential to make an eternal difference in a person's life, and that God can give back to us a bountiful harvest on our seeds of kindness.

Anxiety in a man's heart weighs it down, but an encouraging word makes it glad.

—*Proverbs* 12:25 AMP

Day 6 — The Fruit of Righteousness

Day 6

Read *But seek first the kingdom of God and His righteousness, and all these things shall be added to you* (Matthew 6:33).

Then justice will dwell in the wilderness, and righteousness remain in the fruitful field. The work of righteousness will be peace, and the effect of righteousness, quietness and assurance forever. My people will dwell in a peaceful habitation, in secure dwellings, and in quiet resting places (Isaiah 32:16–18).

According to Matthew 6:33, as we seek first God's kingdom and His righteousness—which is His way of doing things—then all those things we have need of are supposed to be added unto us. And one of the right ways of doing, to me, is to be fervent rather than lazy in our prayer life. Then, as Isaiah 32:16–18 says, in our "sowing" of God's right ways of doing things, we can begin to receive the result of living in a peaceful habitation, in secure dwellings, and in quiet resting places. What a reward for doing things God's way!

Let's look closer at the passage of scripture in Isaiah chapter 32:16–18, which says, "The effect—or fruit—of righteousness is quietness and assurance forever." Hallelujah! That's pretty plain, isn't it? Our righteousness, our right-standing with God, can bring us peace. If we tap into God's ways of doing things and His way of being, when we align ourselves with His Word and His will, His peace can follow us and fill our lives.

Now, Isaiah 32:9–15 also has an unusual passage on idleness, which shows the net result of doing nothing—which yields nothing—and doing much, which yields much more.

This principle can apply to any area of life. But let's look at it from the standpoint of spiritual idleness or laziness. Remember the old saying: "No prayer, no power. Little prayer, little power. Much prayer, much power." Well, if Luke 6:38 is correct, which tells us that as we give, it's given back to us good measure, pressed down, shaken together, and running over, then it would seem logical that we must give God something to work with to get into the "running over" return stage. As Galatians 6:7 KJV says, *Be not deceived; God is not mocked: for whatsoever a man soweth, that shall he also reap.*

"…it would seem logical that we must give God something to work with to get into the 'running over' return stage."

The work of righteousness will be peace, and the effect of righteousness, quietness and assurance forever.

—Isaiah 32:17

So, as we look at Isaiah chapter 32 from a spiritual perspective, it can encourage us to be diligent in our prayer life. We can choose faithfulness over idleness or laziness in prayer and reap the fruit of our efforts.

Pray Consider praying this prayer...

Heavenly Father, we thank You for Your Word, which says, Now may He who supplies seed to the sower, and bread for food, supply and multiply the seed you have sown and increase the fruits of your righteousness (2 Corinthians 9:10). As we read and study Your Word, and as we continue to walk in agreement with Your ways of doing things, we pray that You will help us to experience Your supernatural peace like never before. We pray that You provide us with plenty of seed to sow, and as we sow our seed, we trust that the fruit of our righteousness would be increased, according to Your Word. In Jesus' name, amen.

But seek first the kingdom of God and His righteousness, and all these things shall be added to you.

–Matthew 6:33

Obey Consider this…

I believe there's something about taking a step of obedience to God that can make all the difference in the situations you face. It can open doors and change things, and I believe God honors obedience. But I'm not asking you to obey me—I'm asking you to obey God. Consider planting a seed according to the Bible (Luke 6:38, Malachi 3:10–11) into your church or into a ministry that you are partners with. Why not pray for them? And if you can do something else for them, consider doing so. I encourage you to ask God to bless your seed sown, and expect a miracle harvest in the area you need it most. If you need prayer or would like to be a partner with this ministry, you can go online at oralroberts.com or call the Abundant Life® Prayer Group at 918-495-7777.

Day 7 *Unequally Yoked*

Read *Do not be unequally yoked… [do not make mismated alliances…inconsistent with your faith]. For what partnership have right living and right standing with God with iniquity and lawlessness? Or how can light have fellowship with darkness* (2 Corinthians 6:14 AMP)?

What does it mean to be *unequally yoked*? Well, let's first look at what it means to be *yoked*. If we look at this word as it concerns animals, such as horses or oxen, a *yoke* is a type of harness that ties two animals together to combine their pulling strength. It joins them at the neck so they can work together as a team.

My Grandpa Charlie showed me this principle very clearly when I was young. I learned from him that when you yoke two horses together, it's important that the yoke fits them properly. If the yoke fits, the animals can carry the burden evenly. If not, then it can injure the animal. The yoke must fit properly to be a lighter burden. He was convinced that if two animals were unevenly yoked, as the stronger animal pulled forward, it could break its neck because the weight was unevenly distributed and the stronger animal was carrying a load it was not meant to carry.

I believe our lives can be so much closer to God when we link ourselves to people who build us up instead of tearing us down. Perhaps this is why God is telling us through this verse of scripture that it is vital that we connect ourselves with people who will sharpen us *as iron sharpens iron* (Proverbs 27:17).

Jesus talked about His yoke also. In 1 Peter 5:7, He said for us to cast our cares on Him. Why? Well, I personally believe He is well able to carry every care we have. It's not that we don't do our part, but once we've done what we are supposed to do in a situation, then we can join ourselves or yoke ourselves to Jesus, to the Word, and to the power in that Word to build us up.

Then as we see in Matthew 11:30, His yoke is easy—meaning that it fits. So as we join with Jesus and do it according to His Word and His will, can you see that He is well able to make the burden light? This sounds like supernatural teamwork to me.

"This sounds like supernatural teamwork to me."

Give all your worries and cares to God, for he cares about you.

–1 Peter 5:7 NLT

This does not mean that we don't live in the world, because the Bible says in John 17:14–15 that we do! Even though we are "in" it, we don't have to be totally dependent and totally hooked up with the world only. For example, I have had acquaintances and people I work with and encounter through the daily experiences of my life who are "in the world." But as a Christian, I also have a supernatural source I can go to when I need help. When it comes to "joining myself in the spirit" with One who can help me spiritually deal with the daily load of life, the way I see it, that person should be Jesus—My burden-bearer and burden-sharer, my Savior, and my source of peace. I can't cast *my* part on Him because I have to do my part. But the burden of what I face daily belongs to Jesus, the burden-bearer.

I believe it is so important to yoke ourselves to the scriptural Source of power—Jesus Christ Himself. He tells us, *Take My yoke upon you and learn from Me, for I am gentle…and you will find rest for your souls. For My yoke is easy and My burden is light* (Matthew 11:29–30). The way I understand the Bible, when we yoke ourselves to the Lord, we can harness ourselves into His purpose and plan for our lives, we can connect ourselves to His unlimited mercy, love, and faithfulness, and we can plug into His power source that can bring about His victory in our lives, in Jesus' name.

"I believe it is so important to yoke ourselves to the scriptural Source of power— Jesus Christ Himself."

Pray Consider praying this prayer…
Dear Lord, we come before You now in the name of Jesus, and we ask You to show us if there are areas of our lives where we are unequally yoked to a source of power other than You. And we ask You for wisdom and guidance on how to make the corrections we may need to make. By faith, we yoke ourselves to You, Father God. And we thank You for sharing our burdens as we rely on You and stand on the promises in Your Word. In Jesus' name, amen.

Obey Consider this…

So how do we put this principle into practice? How do we recognize if we are being unequally yoked or leaving the Lord out of some area in our lives? I think the best answer is found in the following verse: *If any of you lacks wisdom, you should ask God, who gives generously to all without finding fault, and it will be given to you* (James 1:5 NIV). If we don't know what to do, we have only to ask! Our Father God is so rich in love and mercy, and I believe He is faithful to answer us when we call on Him.

I also encourage you to call the Abundant Life® Prayer Group at any time, day or night (918-495-7777) and ask them to join their faith with yours as you expect a miracle.

Take My yoke upon you and learn from Me, for I am gentle…and you will find rest for your souls. For My yoke is easy and My burden is light.

—Matthew 11:29–30

Day 8 · Set Free

Read The thief comes only in order to steal and kill and destroy. I came that they may have and enjoy life, and have it in abundance (to the full, till it overflows) (John 10:10 AMP).

The word *deliverance* can make us think of negative images like something out of a scary movie, but deliverance simply means "the act of setting a person free." We can be delivered from sin, sickness, disease, depression, fear, anxiety, financial challenges, broken relationships; and the list goes on. I believe we can be delivered from anything that is unlike the abundant life that John 10:10 promises us, through the blood of Jesus and the power of His never-changing Word.

So, why would Christians need deliverance and restoration? Well, as my father-in-law, Oral, used to say, "God is a good God, and the devil is a bad devil." James 1:17 tells us that every good and perfect gift comes from the Father. John 10:10 says that Satan comes to steal, kill, and destroy, while Jesus came to give us life. So, there is a spiritual war going on, and the devil may try to cause us trouble. But when he does, the Bible says God is on our side to help set us free!

"The name of Jesus is our powerful deliverer, as the Word of God reminds us. "

Jesus said in Luke 10:19 AMP that He gives us authority and power *over all the power that the enemy possesses; and nothing shall in any way harm us.* He called us to be the head and not the tail, to be above and not beneath (Deuteronomy 28:13). The name of Jesus is our powerful deliverer, as the Word of God reminds us. We can be bold in our faith because God is with us and He can always help us.

I believe the Heavenly Father, Who always goes above and beyond what we can ask or think, wants to restore us completely. Ephesians 3:20 says that He wants to do exceedingly abundantly beyond what we can ask or think. I don't know about you, but there are a lot of things I can think of to expand the kingdom of God. So, I believe God want us to think big, do great things, and as the Lord's prayer says in Matthew 6, deliver us from the evil things that have tried to destroy our lives.

Pray Consider praying this prayer…

Heavenly Father, we thank You for sending Your Son to the cross to redeem us and restore us to right relationship with You and for all the blessings Jesus purchased for us through the cross. We thank You that through the shed blood of Jesus, we can have power over the works of the devil. God, we pray for You to bless us and help us to enjoy the abundant life Jesus came to give to us, according to John 10:10. In the name of Jesus and according to God's Word, we rebuke the devil and command him to take his hands off of God's property. We pray for God's supernatural deliverance from any challenges we may be facing. In Jesus' name, amen.

Obey Consider this…

What challenge are you facing today? What obstacle is blocking your path to victory? Consider writing it down, holding it up before you, and speaking these words over it: "Obstacle (name the situation), I say in the name of Jesus that I am determined to fulfill the Word of God in my life. I am more than a conqueror through Christ Jesus, in Jesus' name!" Now, tear up that piece of paper as a point of contact to release your faith for God's delivering and restoring power to cover your situation and turn things around for your good as you do your part according to God's Word.

Day 9 — The Double Miracle of Forgiveness

Read Whenever you stand praying, if you have anything against anyone, forgive him… (Mark 11:25).

When we are hurt by someone, it's amazingly easy to hold on to the offense. But when we forgive the one who has wronged us, not only can that person be released, in my opinion, to the most awesome power on earth—the love of God—but we also put ourselves in a scriptural position to allow God to restore our souls in a way that only He can do.

"What does the Bible say? Does God require us to forgive in order to be forgiven? And if so, is it possible to forgive?"

But you may say, "Lindsay, you don't know my story. You don't know what I went through and how hard it is for me." Well, I certainly have a story too, and forgiving was extremely hard for me, so I understand what it's like. But I want to ask you a question: What does the Bible say? Does God require us to forgive in order to be forgiven? And if so, is it possible to forgive?

Mark 11:25–26 says, *Whenever you stand praying, if you have anything against anyone, forgive him, that your Father in heaven may also forgive you your trespasses. But if you do not forgive, neither will your Father in heaven forgive your trespasses.* But is it really possible to forgive those who have deeply wronged you? Consider this:

One of the greatest examples I've ever heard of forgiveness in the face of terrible hurt is the story of a precious lady named Anita and what she was able to do *through Christ who gave her strength* (Philippians 4:13). Several years after Anita's father was murdered, one of the men who killed him was transferred to the prison where she was working as a chaplain. But rather than asking to be transferred to another prison, as many people in her position would have done, Anita asked to have a meeting with the man.

"I thought the least I could do," she says, "was ask him if he knew the Lord as his personal Savior."

What she didn't know was that during this man's previous years of imprisonment, he had accepted Christ as his Savior, stopped abusing drugs and alcohol, and had joined a prison job-training program. And one of the things he wanted desperately was the opportunity to ask for Anita's forgiveness. As they met for the first time, the man began telling her how sorry he was for what had happened. And as he spoke, Anita felt the Holy Spirit prompting her to forgive him and release him from the guilt he was carrying.

"It was like I could see something just lift off of him," Anita said. "I didn't realize until later that when he was released from the guilt, I was released from all the hatred and bitterness I was carrying around inside me."

If ever there was a testimony of unconditional love and absolute forgiveness, I believe this is it. There's no way to describe what Anita must have been feeling when she went to work that day and ran face-first into the worst nightmare she could possibly ever imagine.

The emotion she must have felt for the man who killed her father would seem to be beyond description. And to find the ability—through the power of God—to release him from what he had done was nothing short of miraculous. But also to be released from what she was carrying inside herself was really miraculous. I'd have to call that a double healing—a double miracle of forgiveness!

And just as we see Anita reaching out to God to make this extraordinary act of forgiveness possible, I believe we, too, can reach out to Him for all that we have need of. And as we do, I believe God can take our lives into the place of the extraordinary, just as He did for Anita.

Now to Him who is able to do exceedingly abundantly above all that we ask or think, according to the power that works in us, to Him be glory in the church by Christ Jesus to all generations, forever and ever. Amen.

—Ephesians 3:20-21

Pray Consider praying this prayer…

*Heavenly Father, in the name of Jesus, I submit to Your Word on forgiveness. And as tough and seemingly impossible as it may appear, I am believing that **through Christ, all things are possible,** according to Matthew 19:26. Thank You, Lord, for helping me to be obedient to Your Word. And as I do what Your will and Your Word says, I thank You for doing **exceedingly abundantly above all I can ask or think,** according to Ephesians 3:20. In Jesus' name, amen.*

Obey Consider this…

Now, here's just a thought for you to consider. If you recognize that any of these feelings related to unforgiveness, offense, or hurt may be holding you back from your full potential in Christ, I encourage you to start releasing the "baggage," so to speak, as God directs. Even if you start with baby steps, I believe that as you start to move in obedience to God's Word to forgive, you can walk right into His double miracle of forgiveness for your life.

Prospering in All Things

Read *Beloved, I pray that you may prosper in all things and be in health, just as your soul prospers* (3 John 2).

What an amazing scripture 3 John 2 is! It has changed the course of my life, and this is also the verse that changed the life of my father-in-law, Oral. He often told the story of how he and Evelyn were living in Enid, Oklahoma, where he was pastoring a little church while going to school. Evelyn was home with two young children. Richard wasn't even born yet. They had almost no money and they struggled just to buy groceries and put gas in their little "rattletrap" car, as he called it.

But thank the Lord, Oral made a habit every morning of reading a passage of Scripture and having a time of prayer before he left home each day.

One morning, he was in a hurry and he left the house without reading the Scriptures. He ran back into the house and grabbed his Bible, which fell open to 3 John 2. He was astonished to read the verse, because of the word *prosper*. So he read the verse to Evelyn, who said, "Oral, is that really in the Bible?" Before that day, they had never believed God wanted His people to prosper—and yet there it was in God's Word. As Oral said about that day, "I had a decision to make because the pastor of our church didn't preach prosperity." And he continued by saying that his point was that *he* was the pastor who didn't preach it!

Oral stayed home that entire day reading and studying what he believed to be a life-changing revelation that God wants His people to prosper in every area of life. And as they say, the rest is history! Can you imagine what they could have missed out on if they hadn't had that amazing revelation?

Beloved, I pray that you may prosper in all things and be in health, just as your soul prospers.

—3 John 2

Prosperity means "to have a prosperous journey." In 3 John 2, it also means "to be fortunate or successful, bringing something good of physical and spiritual health." What an amazing blessing from the Lord! Imagine what this kind of prosperity might look like in our lives as we reach out in faith to God to receive it. Imagine what our lives can be like as God helps us to be successful in all things.

If you've never considered God to be a source of help in this way, I want to remind you that the Bible calls the Holy Spirit the divine Paraclete—which means "the one called alongside to help." So, not only can "help be on the way," but it can be the spiritual help of the Holy Spirit to join in and to assist you in your journey through daily life. Praise the Lord for His goodness!

Pray Consider praying this prayer…
Father God, I thank You that You put 3 John 2 in the Bible and that prospering and being in health are also part of Your plan for a successful journey. I thank You that according to this scripture, You want to bless and prosper me in every area of my life, and I thank You that Psalm 35:27 says that You delight in the prosperity of Your people. I declare Your Word that tells me I am to be healed by Jesus' stripes (1 Peter 2:24). Thank You for sending the Holy Spirit into my life to help me daily. I thank You so much for all the good things You've brought into my life, and I give You all the praise and glory. In Jesus' name, amen!

Obey

Consider this...

Consider asking the Lord to begin to show you areas of your life where you have not been enjoying all that He has for you. When He speaks to you about areas where you can have more of His abundance, provision, and health, you can begin to speak 3 John 2 over those areas of your life, believing that as you sow into God's kingdom (Luke 6:38), you have a covenant right to receive a harvest back from Him. Begin to expect to see growth and change as your life lines up with what God says. And give Him praise for His Word coming to pass in your life.

Give, and it will be given to you: good measure, pressed down, shaken together, and running over will be put into your bosom. For with the same measure that you use, it will be measured back to you.

–Luke 6:38

Day 11 — Staying in God's Secret Place

Read *He that dwelleth in the secret place of the most High shall abide under the shadow of the Almighty. I will say of the Lord, He is my refuge and my fortress: my God; in him will I trust* (Psalm 91:1–2 KJV).

Psalm 91 is a beautiful passage of Scripture, showing what we might call the all-encompassing protection that God makes known to His children. According to this Psalm, His protection is available to us morning, noon, and night, in sickness and health, in good times, in challenging times, no matter what we may be facing. I believe the Word of God makes it clear that we can always call on Him; we can always apply His Word according to the faith in our heart.

Now, I personally find it such a relief to know, without a doubt, that the Lord desires to keep my family and me under His shadow or spiritual covering. But I want to draw your attention to something important that I believe we are called to do if we want to take part in what God has for us in Psalm 91. We have a part to play if we want to tap into the Word available to us, according to these verses. And we can see what our responsibility is by breaking down a few of the words in Psalm 91:1–2.

First of all, I believe that if we want to have the Almighty God's protective power working for ourselves and our loved ones, then we need to pay attention to His instruction to *abide under His shadow.* So, let's consider this question: What does it mean to abide in Him?

Well, the word *abide* means to "live in, remain, and find rest and peace." That leads me to believe that abiding in the Lord isn't something we do on a casual basis, once in a while, half-heartedly. Rather, I believe it is something that we diligently, fervently choose to do every day. In the face of difficult people, confusing situations, stressful emotions, evil reports, financial distress, or any of the other issues of life that can get us overwhelmed, I believe it's important to decide daily to *remain* in faith, planted firmly in what God's Word says to us. And as we stay put in God by continuing to pray, praise, worship, speak His Word, believe His Word, release our faith and expect a miracle over our situation, He can cover us with His protective shadow, covering us like a shade keeps us safe from the burning sun in the heat of summer.

Second, I believe Psalm 91 points out the safekeeping that we can rest in as we trust God and declare His promises as a confession of our faith. When we *trust* in the Lord, we "have confidence" in Him—we can have peace in the midst of any storm, because we're connected to His protective power according to the Bible. We can trust in Him completely, as we abide in Him according to His Word: *The Lord is faithful, who will establish you and guard you from the evil one* (2 Thessalonians 3:3).

"We can trust in Him completely, as we abide in Him according to His Word…"

I believe that the Lord desires to be our refuge and our strong tower. Psalm 46:1 says, *God is our refuge and strength, a very present help in trouble.* That's an important promise because the world seems to be full of trouble. In fact, in John 16:33 Jesus says, *"In the world you will have tribulation; but be of good cheer, I have overcome the world."*

How important it can be these days to be connected to the One who has overcome the troubles of this world. I encourage you to make that choice to connect with God every day, as often as it comes to mind. Open your life to God's Word and His promises to care for you, and I believe you can begin to see situations turn around for your good!

Pray Consider praying this prayer...

In Jesus' name, we declare by faith that along with our loved ones, we enjoy peaceful, happy, healthy lives. We pray that no accident, injury, attack, or sickness will be able to prevail over us. We turn that job of safekeeping over to You, Lord, according to Psalm 91, and pray that we can rest in the center of Your protection in every area of life. We ask, Lord, that no evil befalls our homes, our cars, our workplaces, or any of the places we spend time. According to Your Word in Isaiah 54:17, we ask You, Lord, and declare that no weapon formed against us shall prosper. Thank You that we can ask You to protect us in our physical body, mind, emotional well-being, finances, godly relationships, and everything else that concerns us, as well as our loved ones. And thank You for Your promise to give us abundant life through Your Son, Jesus. Show us Your abundance every day, in every way, so that we can have peace in our lives and be a blessing to others. In Jesus' name, amen.

Obey

There is something about hearing myself speak God's Word in faith over my life that can cause faith to rise up on the inside of me for the needs I may face in my life. So, I encourage you, too, to find ways to keep God's Word before you, so that you can speak it and pray it over and over. You might even consider making a list of favorite verses to keep in your handbag or Bible. Or perhaps write out the verses and hang them up in places where you'll see them often, such as your bathroom mirror or the refrigerator door. As you make it your habit to regularly choose to remain in God's Word and to declare it in faith over your life, I pray you can find yourself abiding under His shadow, trusting in Him, and seeing His miraculous power do wonders for you and your loved ones.

The Lord is faithful,
who will establish you
and guard you from the evil one.

–2 Thessalonians 3:3

Day 12
It's Not as Bad as You Think

Read *If God is for us, who can be against us? He who did not spare His own Son, but delivered Him up for us all, how shall He not with Him also freely give us all things (Romans 8:31–32)?*

Have you ever felt unfairly labeled, misunderstood, or rejected? I believe we all experience thoughts or feelings like that at some point in our lives. It appears that we live in a world where bad news gets magnified, while good news often gets downplayed, or even ignored. But I'm encouraged because as Christians, I think we can have the ultimate and best source of good news that there ever was and ever will be—and that's the Word of God, which contains every bit of good news God felt we would need to live successfully for Him.

So, I thank God for His Word every day! To me, it's filled with His encouraging truth about who we are through the work that Jesus Christ is doing in our lives. As we apply His Word to our lives, we can grow in our faith and find strength in Him, even when faced with challenges.

I believe Jesus Christ exemplifies this truth better than anyone. During His ministry on earth, He received many questions and criticisms, so He knows what it is like when we feel rejected. Just in John chapter 7 alone, we can read many of the negative things that people said about Him, and some of the evil plans they had for Him, such as…

The religious leaders of the day wanted to kill Him (John 7:1). His brothers did not believe in Him (John 7:5). Many people hated Him (John 7:7). He was accused of deliberately deceiving the people in order to take advantage of them (John 7:12). Some people thought He was demon-possessed (John 7:20). They questioned His origin (John 7:27). Some, thankfully, saw that God was with Him and believed on Him (John 7:31). Eventually, He was executed by crucifixion, a death penalty that the Romans reserved for the worst of rebels and criminals.

Jesus faced a lot of challenges. But the labels people tried to put on Him didn't stop Him because He knew who He was, and He knew what He was on this earth to accomplish. He knew what His Father God said about Him: *This is My beloved Son, in whom I am well pleased* (Matthew 3:17). He knew that He was the Son of God, the Messiah, come to save the world from sin.

I believe it is God's opinion that matters most in our life. Knowing who He says we are can set us free from the hurts of rejection. To me, God is the one who determines who I am, who I can be, and what I can do through Him. The Bible says if God is for us, then who can be against us (Romans 8:31)? If we, in faith, turn to God for His help no matter what we face, then I believe He can be the final authority in our situation. His Word can rule over our life, and we can triumph through Him in all things. And to that I say, praise God! Yes, Lord!

"God is the one who determines who I am, who I can be, and what I can do through Him."

I am convinced that one simple word from God about who we are in Him can put us on the right road today, and it can change the course of our entire life. Failures, labels, mistakes, or unkind words from unkind people, no matter how awful, do not have to hold us down…not if we know who we are in Christ. Remember this: in spite of all the negative things that people said about Jesus, He was exactly who God said He was—the Christ, the Son of God! He was raised from the dead, in victory over sin and the devil. Difficult times didn't defeat Jesus, and they don't have to defeat us either. Through Him, we can rise above the labels, the devastation, or any other situations we may face, and believe for the victory He achieved for us on the cross.

"Difficult times didn't defeat Jesus, and they don't have to defeat us either."

Pray Consider praying this prayer…
Heavenly Father, thank You for showing us what Jesus endured. Just as He stayed true to His calling and accomplished what You sent Him here to do, we ask You to help us realize what You have called each of us to do, and we commit to doing our very best to follow You and the example that Jesus set for us. Help us to focus on the truth of who we are in Christ, according to Your Word. In Jesus' name, amen.

Obey   Consider this...
I encourage you to really dwell on 1 John 4:4, which declares, *You are of God, little children.* You are the essence and nature and character of God, wonderfully made in the image of God (Genesis 1:27). You may choose to think about what you can do to really succeed and thrive in this world, and in all the Lord has called you to do and be. I encourage you to ask Him to show you His purpose for your life. And as He reveals that to you, I encourage you to step out in faith and put your gifts and talents to use for Him. I believe that as you see who you are in Christ, God can use you for His Kingdom and not only cause your gifts to bless others, but He can bless you mightily in return as well.

You are of God, little children, and have overcome them, because He who is in you is greater than he who is in the world.

−1 John 4:4

Day 13 *From Devastation to Restoration*

Read *Joseph, being seventeen years old, was feeding the flock with his brothers. And the lad was with the sons of Bilhah and the sons of Zilpah, his father's wives; and Joseph brought a bad report of them to his father. Now Israel [Jacob] loved Joseph more than all his children, because he was the son of his old age. Also he made him a tunic of many colors. But when his brothers saw that their father loved him more than all his brothers, they hated him and could not speak peaceably to him* (Genesis 37:2–4).

Can you imagine having a houseful of brothers who could not even speak peaceably to you? How lonely and sad that kind of situation must be! And for Joseph, things just went from bad to worse.

"I believe that by holding onto God's promises, Joseph was able to have what we call his 'from the pit to the palace' experience."

Now Joseph had a dream, and he told it to his brothers; and they hated him even more. So he said to them, "Please hear this dream which I have dreamed: There we were, binding sheaves in the field. Then behold, my sheaf arose and also stood upright; and indeed your sheaves stood all around and bowed down to my sheaf." And his brothers said to him, "Shall you indeed reign over us? Or shall you indeed have dominion over us?" So they hated him even more for his dreams and for his words (Genesis 37:5–8).

Eventually, Joseph's angry brothers left him alone in a pit to die. He was pulled out of the pit, brought to the land of Egypt, and sold into slavery. Then, through no fault of his own, Joseph found himself falsely accused and he wound up in prison. Through a series of events that only the hand of God could orchestrate, Joseph eventually ended up freed from prison, taken out of slavery, and given a place in the Pharaoh's palace, in a position of great importance, with the ability to literally save the nation from a deadly drought. God used Joseph to save a nation from starving to death.

Then he dreamed still another dream and told it to his brothers, and said, "Look, I have dreamed another dream. And this time, the sun, the moon, and the eleven stars bowed down to me."

–Genesis 37:9

Can you imagine the loneliness and discouragement Joseph must have felt, and what it took for him to believe God's promise in spite of what the circumstances looked like? I believe that by holding onto God's promises, Joseph was able to have what we call his "from the pit to the palace" experience.

And just like Joseph, who went from the pit to the prison to the palace, I believe that God has miracles of restoration for all of us. I choose to believe that we are not hopeless; rather, I believe that God has hope for us all, even when we may not feel like it. In 3 John 2, it says that God's highest and greatest desire is for us to prosper and be in health, even as our soul prospers. And Acts 10:34 KJV says that He is *no respecter of persons.* This leads me to believe that if God can turn Joseph's life around for good, He can do it for you as you reach out to Him in faith, believing for His miracle-working power to transform your situation and bring about good for you.

*Beloved,
I pray that you may
prosper in all things and be in health,
just as your soul prospers.*

—3 John 1:2

Pray Consider praying this prayer...

Father God, we thank You for showing us, through the miraculous journey of Joseph, that no matter what we face, Your restoration power can be there for us if we trust You, have faith in Your Word, and do not give up. Show me Your miracle-working power today and every day, in big ways and small ways, as I walk with You and trust in You. Thank You for bringing me through any and all difficult situations, and for bringing me restoration and hope. In Jesus' name, amen.

Obey Consider this...

I think that one of the best ways to get out of our own thoughts and stop focusing on our own problems is to read someone else's story. Then after that, we can see how God brings things together for good, just like He did for Joseph. When it seemed that Joseph's life was over, through God he was rescued, exalted, and gloriously restored with his family. The way I see it, when God does the restoring, it's just so much better than we can imagine. Consider reading Joseph's entire story in the book of Genesis, starting in chapter 37, and pay special attention to how God brought him through to victory, despite all sorts of challenges. I believe it will be a blessing to you!

"...when God does the restoring, it's just so much better than we can imagine."

Day 14 · The "Sozo" Life

Read *Sozo: (Greek root) to save, deliver, protect, heal, preserve, do well, be whole, make whole**

Sozo is a Greek word that is used over 100 times in the New Testament. According to *Strong's Greek Dictionary,* sozo means to save, keep safe and sound, rescue, deliver, heal, make whole, and preserve. To me, the writers of the New Testament revealed the completeness of what it means to be saved by using sozo in different contexts to refer to each aspect of salvation. So, let's look at some verses describing these different aspects of the concept of sozo, according to the Bible.

"...sozo means to save, keep safe and sound, rescue, deliver, heal, make whole, and preserve."

First of all, sozo means salvation: *For the Son of Man has come to seek and to save (sozo) that which was lost* (Luke 19:10). Another verse is Romans 10:9: *That if you confess with your mouth the Lord Jesus and believe in your heart that God has raised Him from the dead, you will be saved (sozo).*

Sozo also means healing: *But Jesus turned around, and when He saw her He said, "Be of good cheer, daughter; your faith has made you well (sozo)." And the woman was made well (sozo) from that hour* (Matthew 9:22). Another healing verse is Acts 14:9–10: *This man heard Paul speaking. Paul, observing him intently and seeing that he had faith to be healed (sozo), said with a loud voice, "Stand up straight on your feet!" And he leaped and walked.*

*Definition taken from Strong's Exhaustive Concordance of the Bible, Greek dictionary entry 4982

And sozo means deliverance: *Those who had seen it reported to them how the man who was demon-possessed had been made well (sozo)* (Luke 8:36 NASB).

God anointed Jesus of Nazareth with the Holy Spirit and with power, who went about doing good and healing all who were oppressed by the devil, for God was with Him.

—Acts 10:38

I think it is obvious from these verses that God desires for people to be completely whole. In studying this small but power-packed Greek word, we can have a little deeper understanding of what Jesus has done for us. I think God is showing us that sozo, the wholeness that I believe the Lord wants us to walk in, is the opposite of any destruction that the devil may try to bring upon us. I believe the sozo life can free us from the grip of the devil's destruction, torment, and overpowering burdens, and it can be available to us as we call on God according to His Word, and in faith cast our cares on Him. As we do what the Bible tells us to do, then according to His Word and His will, we can begin to walk in the sozo life Jesus purchased for us on the cross.

The Bible says in Acts 10:38 that *God anointed Jesus of Nazareth with the Holy Spirit and with power, who went about doing good and healing all who were oppressed by the devil, for God was with Him.* Jesus went about giving sozo life to people He came in contact with. Through His shed blood on the cross, He gave salvation, healing, and deliverance to all who would come to Him. You see, sozo is not just wholeness, but it is the opposite of every form of satan's destruction. So the big question is, are we letting the Lord bring that into our lives daily? Are we sharing it with others? As for me and my house, we choose the sozo life, and I encourage you to do the same!

Pray Consider praying this prayer...

Heavenly Father, I thank You for sending Your precious Son to this earth and paying the price on the cross for our salvation. And I thank You that during His earthly ministry, Jesus demonstrated to us by how He ministered to the people that that's how You would have us live. You want us to have sozo life—saved, healed, and delivered from all the works of the enemy, the devil. In the name of Jesus, we expect miracles to come into our lives as we release our faith. Thank You, Lord! Amen.

Obey Consider this...

Now that you have an opportunity to see what this sozo gift can mean in your life, I want to encourage you to really study these scriptures and then consider letting the principles of these gifts begin to be shared through your life. As it says in Matthew 10:8, *Freely you have received, freely give.* Since Jesus has already given of Himself, perhaps now it's our turn to begin to give of ourselves. I encourage you to take a moment to look at your surroundings and see if the Lord is asking you to reach out and be a part of His extended hand as God leads. Then, as your life becomes full in the Lord, allow the overflow of your life to become a blessing to someone else.

For the Son of Man has come to seek and to save that which was lost.

–Luke 19:10

Day 15 — The Miracle of Seed Faith

Read As evening approached, the disciples came to him and said, "This is a remote place, and it's already getting late. Send the crowds away, so they can go to the villages and buy themselves some food." Jesus replied, "They do not need to go away. You give them something to eat." "We have here only five loaves of bread and two fish," they answered. "Bring them here to me," he said. And he directed the people to sit down on the grass. Taking the five loaves and the two fish and looking up to heaven, he gave thanks and broke the loaves. Then he gave them to the disciples, and the disciples gave them to the people. They all ate and were satisfied, and the disciples picked up twelve basketfuls of broken pieces that were left over. The number of those who ate was about five thousand men, besides women and children (Matthew 14:15–21 NIV).

One of my favorite miracle stories in the Bible is the miracle of the feeding of the 5,000 with the little boy's lunch of loaves and fishes. Can you imagine how much food it would take to feed 5,000 men, not including the women and children who were with them? What kind of miracle would that take? While I was reading this amazing story of God's multiplying power, I felt the strongest impression that the Lord was saying to me that this was an "astronomical miracle."

I couldn't wait to see exactly what the word meant. I had a pretty good idea, but I felt it was going to mean something special to me according to this passage of scripture. When I looked up the word *astronomical* in the dictionary, I began to laugh because the meaning was so perfect for this situation described in Matthew 14:15–21. Astronomical means enormously or inconceivably large. Enormously means excessively, vastly, and exceptionally. Inconceivably means unbelievably, incapable of being imagined or grasped, and so unlikely it is thought impossible. So, to really understand what the Lord was impressing on my heart regarding the real meaning of this miracle, I came to see that it was an "astronomical miracle!"

The miracle wasn't just stretching one little boy's lunch to feed three or four people; it was multiplying a lunch far beyond what is humanly possible, resulting in enough food for a crowd when there was originally only enough food to feed a few. In my opinion, this miracle shows the essence of the Biblical principle of seed faith.

So, what is seed faith? To me, the miracle of seed faith is one of the most straightforward concepts in the world. Just look at a farmer as an example of how simple seed faith is. The farmer plants seeds to get a certain crop, such as corn. He carefully tends the seeds, and then he reaps the harvest of what he planted. If he planted corn, he'll get corn.

It's the same with us. The Bible assures us in Galatians 6:7, *Do not be deceived, God is not mocked; for whatever a man sows, that he will also reap.* Now, in our natural minds, we can see that if we plant tomato seeds, we will reap tomatoes, but can you also see that if we plant nothing, we reap nothing? But it's not just the planting. We also can see in Luke 6:38 the astronomical multiplying power of God—*Give, and it will be given to you: good measure, pressed down, shaken together, and running over...*

In the story of the feeding of the 5,000, what also stands out to me—what I think is so important—is that the little boy gave. By giving his lunch to the Master, the little boy planted a seed to God, and according to this passage of Scripture, we can clearly see the miraculous harvest that followed. And here is a passing thought... the Bible says there were twelve baskets of food left over after everyone was fed. I wonder who got the twelve baskets? My first thought is that they went to the little boy who gave up his lunch as a seed to the Lord (John 6:9).

> "I believe that God not only wants us in the 'good measure and pressed down' stage, but that He also wants us in the 'running over' part as well."

Imagine the multiplying power of our seed growing into an overflowing, abundant, astronomical harvest. I believe that God not only wants us in the "good measure and pressed down" stage, but that He also wants us in the "running over" part as well. He put it in His Word, right? But it's up to us to sow or not to sow. And when we sow, we can sow in obedience to what God tells us in our heart. We can also keep in mind God's mathematics in 2 Corinthians 9:6, which tell us when we sow sparingly, we reap sparingly, and when we sow bountifully, we reap bountifully!

When we give something to the Lord to work with that He can bless and multiply, I believe we are planting a seed into the good soil of His kingdom. Personally, giving brings me great joy and satisfaction. But scripturally speaking, God says on the other end of giving is receiving. And on the other end of sowing is reaping. I believe that's why He called it seed-time *and* harvest (Genesis 8:22). As I give to God, His Word says that He receives the seed and turns it into a harvest to bless me in return. That is a wonderful example of the nature of God!

Pray Consider praying this prayer...
Father God, we see that it is Your will for us to be cheerful givers according to 2 Corinthians 9:7, which says, So let each one give as he purposes in his heart, not grudgingly or of necessity; for God loves a cheerful giver. So, we commit to You that we will be more aware of giving of ourselves—our love, our compassion, our talent, our finances, our time and effort, and our hugs and smiles to those around us. And Father, as we choose to obey Your Word in seed-faith giving, we now release our faith to expect a divine harvest from You, the Lord of the harvest (Matthew 9:38), in the area where we need it most. In Jesus' name, amen.

Obey Consider this...
Now that you have read about the miracle of seed faith, I encourage you to consider setting your miracle in motion. Malachi 3:10–11 says to bring tithes and offerings into God's storehouse and prove Him to see if He will not open the window of Heaven, pour us out a blessing where there is not enough room to contain it all, and rebuke the devourer for our sake. I encourage you to consider sowing into God's storehouse—God's work that is blessing you and others—whether it's this ministry or somewhere else in God's kingdom. I encourage you to become a sower so that according to God's Word, you can become a reaper. I pray you are sensitive to the leading of the Holy Spirit on this, and whether it's a gift of your time, or money, or help, or whatever it might be, I encourage you to give as unto the Lord, expecting an abundant harvest in your life.

Day 16 Choose Peace

Read Peace I leave with you, My peace I give to you; not as the world gives do I give to you. Let not your heart be troubled; neither let it be afraid (John 14:27).

Have you ever found yourself in the midst of turmoil, and you honestly didn't know which way to turn? I believe it's safe to say that many of us have been there. Richard and I have certainly had our fair share of hardships and heartache. But the sustaining force that has carried us through has always been God's unfailing peace.

"When we choose His life, His ways, and His peace, we can have the blessed assurance that He watches over His own Word to perform it..."

Joshua 24:15 says, *Choose for yourselves this day whom you will serve... But as for me and my house, we will serve the Lord.* Do you remember the game kids play, where someone hides a penny in one hand and places both hands behind their back? You have to pick only one hand to try to find the penny. And you have to stick with your one choice. Well, this concept is the same in choosing peace. Deuteronomy 30:19 says, *I have set before you life and death, blessing and cursing; therefore choose life, that both you and your descendants may live.* The choice is ours, but we do have to *choose.* We can't have both.

Along with the choice we make comes the result it produces. This scripture says that one reason to choose life is so that we not only can live a life in God, but we can also set up that opportunity for our children. When we choose His life, His ways, and His peace, we can have the blessed assurance that He watches over His own Word to perform it (Jeremiah 1:12).

In my opinion, having peace is something we have to actively choose on a daily basis. The economy may look bad, gas prices may seem sky high, and we can go into sticker shock when we see the latest prices at the grocery store. But the Bible says that our Father God can guide and comfort us through the challenges we face. Look at Psalm 34:19—*Many are the afflictions of the righteous, but the Lord delivers him out of them all.* That's good news! The Lord delivered them out of them all! And John 16:33 says something similar—*These things I have spoken to you, that in Me you may have peace. In the world you will have tribulation; but be of good cheer, I have overcome the world.*

Choose for yourselves this day whom you will serve... But as for me and my house, we will serve the Lord.

–Joshua 24:15

Here's one more final thought to encourage you: A friend of mine, Joni Lamb, who is a precious woman of God, sings a song by Geron Davis that has ministered so much to me through some really interesting times, and I believe its message can be a blessing to us all. This song reminds us that Jesus is the "Peace Speaker."* When we

*Geron Davis. "Peace Speaker." ©1989 Meadowgreen Music Company-ASCAP. Administered by EMI CMG Publishing.

go through storms in life, we can feel His peace, which goes beyond our own understanding (Philippians 4:7), because we can have a personal relationship with the Peace Speaker. Jesus doesn't just *give* us peace, but He *pronounces* peace over us. When we have the Peace Speaker on our side, we can be preserved and sustained even through the mightiest storms. As Proverbs 10:25 says, *When the whirlwind passes by, the wicked is no more, but the righteous has an everlasting foundation.*

And the peace of God, which surpasses all understanding, will guard your hearts and minds through Christ Jesus.

—Philippians 4:7

Pray Consider praying this prayer...

Father God, when we find ourselves in the middle of a storm, we commit ourselves to lifting up our hands to You in worship. By faith, we spiritually release any fear that might be holding us back, in Jesus' name, and we choose Your peace. We believe that according to Your Word in Philippians 4:7, Your peace goes beyond our own understanding, and we believe we receive Your peace now to help us stand strong in faith. Thank You for bringing Your peace to us. In Jesus' name, amen.

Obey Consider this...

Whatever storm you may be going through today, I encourage you to call on Jesus, the Peace Speaker, and reach out in faith to Him to meet the needs you are facing. And if you don't truly know Him as the Peace Speaker, or if you have strayed away from Him and want to come back to Him, now can be your time to make what is, in my opinion, one of the most important decisions you'll ever make. You can simply pray, "Father God, I choose to come back to You and Your Son, Jesus, to be the Lord and Savior of my life. Thank You for forgiving my sins and giving me a fresh new start and a new life in the Word. In Jesus' name, amen."

And remember, the prayer partners in the Abundant Life® Prayer Group are available to you day or night, and I encourage you to call 918-495-7777 whenever you want someone to pray with you as you release your faith and expect a miracle.

Day 17 — Knowing Who You Are in Christ

Read *For He made Him who knew no sin to be sin for us, that we might become the righteousness of God in Him* (2 Corinthians 5:21).

What does it mean to be the righteousness of God in Him? If we read this verse in the New Living Translation of the Bible, it makes it so plain—*For God made Christ, who never sinned, to be the offering for our sin, so that we could be made right with God through Christ.* Doesn't it make you feel thankful that we can be made right with God through Christ? It is a comfort to me to know that no matter what happens along our journey of life, the blood of Jesus and His finished work on the cross can enable us to be put back in right-standing with our Father God.

"...our faith in God and His promises to us through Christ has made such a difference in our lives."

So, the righteousness of God in Christ means knowing who God says we are, according to His Word. It's so important to put our trust in that identity in Christ because we live in a world where we face trials and challenges. For Richard and me, our faith in God and His promises to us through Christ has made such a difference in our lives.

So, what does the Bible says about us? As born-again Christians, we are now *in Christ*. According to the Bible, that means we are called to be *overcomers* (Romans 8:37; 1 John 4:4). We are to be *the head and not the tail* (Deuteronomy 28:13), and to *enjoy the fat (the best) of the land* (Genesis

45:18). We have been *bought with a price* (1 Corinthians 6:19–20), *redeemed and forgiven* (Colossians 1:14), and *set apart for God* (Ephesians 1:1–13). We are called to live *free from condemnation* (Romans 8:1–2), *established, anointed, and sealed by God* (2 Corinthians 1:21–22).

We can have *constant access to God through the Holy Spirit* (Ephesians 2:18), and we can be *His ambassadors* on this earth (2 Corinthians 5:20).

Philippians 4:13 tells us that we *can do all things through Christ who strengthens us*, and Romans 8:37 reminds us that *we are more than conquerors through Him who loved us.*

> *For God made Christ, who never sinned, to be the offering for our sin, so that we could be made right with God through Christ.*
>
> —2 Corinthians 5:21 NLT

By accepting the Lord Jesus as our Savior, believing in His Word and receiving it by faith, we can understand and walk in the position of being in right-standing with our

"We can stand up and be strong and confident because we are in Him."

Father God. We can stand up and be strong and confident because we are *in Him*. We are a part of the family of God and entitled to the family benefits that our faith in God's Word provides.

Pray Consider praying this prayer...

Heavenly Father, we thank You that we can be made right with You through Christ Jesus. We thank You for all the precious promises found in Your Word that tell us what our true identity can be. We ask You, Lord, to touch us in every area of our lives. Bless us and keep us, Lord, and make Your face to shine upon us and give us peace, according to Numbers 6:24–26. In Jesus' name, amen.

Obey Consider this…

In my opinion, there is no better way to find out who you are in Christ than to see it according to God's Word. After all, if He created you in His image (Genesis 1:27), shouldn't you go to Him to inquire about who you are in Him? Consider getting out your Bible and your highlighter to look up the verses of scripture that tell you who you are in Christ Jesus. As you find these verses, highlight them, and read them to yourself again and again. As you do this, I believe you can get a new revelation of your identity in Christ Jesus, and I believe you can be a blessing as you begin to see yourself through the eyes of God.

Yet in all these things we are more than conquerors through Him who loved us.

–Romans 8:37

Day 18 — Take the Land

Read Every place on which the sole of your foot treads shall be yours: from the wilderness and Lebanon, from the river, the River Euphrates, even to the Western Sea, shall be your territory (Deuteronomy 11:24).

Every place that the sole of your foot will tread upon I have given you, as I said to Moses (Joshua 1:3).

For all the land which you see I give to you and your descendants forever (Genesis 13:15).

"I felt that the Holy Spirit wanted to teach me about the concept of taking the land..."

Richard and I have a dear pastor friend who was standing in faith to be able to acquire a piece of land that he really believed the Lord wanted him to have for his church's building project. I wanted to join my faith with his, but I sensed in my spirit that I needed to do something more. I felt that the Holy Spirit wanted to teach me about the concept of taking the land, and not just any land or my opinion of what should belong to us, but those things that are set apart as the will of God for us. He began leading me to scriptures such as Deuteronomy 11:24, Joshua 1:3, and Genesis 13:15.

As I began to read and study these scriptures and others, the Holy Spirit spoke to my heart again, this time about a way to actively find a point of contact for my prayer of agreement with my pastor friend. I felt led to actually go to the location that this pastor had his faith set upon and touch the land by faith. That served as my point of contact to pray and believe God for His will to come to pass concerning this land. I prayed in faith that the righteousness of God would prevail in this situation. Richard and I were praying, the pastor and his wife were praying, the congregation was faithfully praying, and we released it to God. Not long after that, the pastor called to tell us that God honored his faith, and the land was theirs.

The Bible teaches in Ephesians 2 that as believers, we have been raised up to sit together in the heavenly places in Christ Jesus. I believe that means we have been given authority, through Jesus, to pray, speak, and act on God's Word, as long as it is in harmony with His will concerning what we are facing. And with this authority, when we know what we are believing for is the will of God and not just an idea of man, we can take the land, so to speak. We can have victory in the situations we face (1 John 5:14-15). And we can receive what we need, in spite of any circumstances that might seem to be saying "no" to us when God says "yes." As 2 Corinthians 5:7 says, *We walk by faith, not by sight.*

I believe it is our responsibility to take our rightful seat of authority according to God's will and Word for our life as we read in Ephesians 2:6, and apply this principle to whatever situation we may find ourselves in. We can spiritually "take the land"...the territory concerning our health, restoration in our families, getting a job, a raise, or a promotion, or any other part of our lives according to our seed, our faith, and the will of God. So I encourage you to search the Bible to find what God desires for you and then stretch out your faith to believe the Word of God concerning His promises for your life.

Pray Consider praying this prayer…

Heavenly Father, please show us the areas in our lives where it is Your will for us to spiritually take the land. We pray that Your precious Holy Spirit would reveal to us the areas in our lives where we need to take the authority You gave us, through the name of Jesus. We ask that You would show us how we can stand on the promises in Your Word regarding the things we need. And as we release our faith in agreement with Your Word and Your will, we believe we can begin to expect miracles in our lives. In Jesus' name, amen.

But God, who is rich in mercy, because of His great love with which He loved us…made us alive together with Christ (by grace you have been saved), and raised us up together, and made us sit together in the heavenly places in Christ Jesus.

– Ephesians 2:4–6

Obey

Now, here comes the fun part. Those of you who know me know I am a big believer in visual aids in my preaching. I like to have something in my hands when I'm talking, and I like to physically do things as a point of contact to demonstrate what I am asking and believing God to do for me. I encourage you to choose a tangible point of contact for your needs too. Why not choose something to signify your prayer need—perhaps a photograph, a scripture, a description of a desired job, or something very simple to serve as a reminder to pray, according to God's will. Then take it in your hands, hold it up before the Lord, and declare in faith: *Lord, as I hold this up before You as a point of contact, I release my faith to You right now and spiritually take this land, according to my seed, my faith, and Your Word and Your will, in the name of Jesus. Amen.*

Day 19 Pray Until the Pain Stops

Read *Keep on asking and it will be given you; keep on seeking and you will find; keep on knocking [reverently] and [the door] will be opened to you. For everyone who keeps on asking receives; and he who keeps on seeking finds; and to him who keeps on knocking, [the door] will be opened. Or what man is there of you, if his son asks him for a loaf of bread, will hand him a stone? Or if he asks for a fish, will hand him a serpent? If you then, evil as you are, know how to give good and advantageous gifts to your children, how much more will your Father Who is in heaven [perfect as He is] give good and advantageous things to those who keep on asking Him* (Matthew 7:7–11 AMP).

When my daughter, Jordan, was about three years old, our family owned a two-door car. One day as we were getting ready to go out, I pulled the driver's seat forward, put her in her car seat, and buckled her in. Then I pushed the driver's seat back and sat down, not realizing that Jordan's little foot was caught in the fold of the seat.

She began to let me know that her foot was in pain, and I instantly realized what I had done. Thankfully, nothing was seriously injured, but she was definitely feeling some discomfort. In the sweetest voice, Jordan cried, "Pray, Mom, pray!" So I started to pray while strapping her back into the seatbelt, and off we went down the road.

We hadn't driven a block when Jordan said, "Pray again, Mom!" I prayed again. Before long she said, "Don't stop! Keep praying, Mom!" After several more blocks of prayer, I finally asked her, "Honey, how many times do you want me to pray?" And with the most serious, determined conviction, she answered, "Pray until the pain stops." Wow, what a concept!

Keep on asking and it will be given you; keep on seeking and you will find; keep on knocking [reverently] and [the door] will be opened to you.

—Matthew 7:7 AMP

Jordan had spoken a truth that can sometimes be easy to forget. Sometimes we have to keep praying until the pain stops. So, we began to pray and thank the Lord for hearing, receiving, and answering our prayers and we stayed in an atmosphere of thanking God. We were not begging, because He never told us to beg. We simply asked, knocked, praised, and received. Seeking God isn't like pressing a button on the microwave. To me, it's diligently and consistently standing in faith until we receive God's answer. I see diligence as meaning to do it, and do it, and *keep on* doing it until our breakthrough

"Seeking God isn't like pressing a button on the microwave... it's diligently and consistently standing in faith until we receive God's answer."

comes. My sweet mother-in-law, Evelyn Roberts, used to call it "praying through."

When we go through a difficult situation, I believe it's important to pray, praise, and be thankful to God that He hears and answers prayer. The Word of God says that you are more than a conqueror in Christ Jesus, spiritually speaking (Romans 8:37), that you are the head and not the tail (Deuteronomy 28:13), and that you can do all things through Christ who strengthens you (Philippians 4:13). And Jeremiah 29:11 says that when you pray, God has good plans to bless you and take care of you.

For I know the thoughts that I think toward you, says the Lord, thoughts of peace and not of evil, to give you a future and a hope.

—Jeremiah 29:11

So, I encourage you to pray and keep on praying, seek and keep on seeking, knock and keep on knocking, until you receive your answer from the Lord who loves you so much.

Pray Consider praying this prayer…
Father God, we thank You that You are the God of miracles. And we thank You that through the finished work of Jesus Christ on the cross, we have authority to stand on Your Word for healing, for financial provision, for peace, and for wholeness in every area of our lives. In Jesus' name, amen.

Obey Consider this…
Whatever challenges you may be facing, I encourage you to take a moment and speak scriptural words of faith over them. And just as my daughter demonstrated, consider "praying until the pain stops." Keep praying. Keep believing. Keep expecting that your miracle is on the way, according to Galatians 6:7,9: *Do not be deceived, God is not mocked; for whatever a man sows, that he will also reap… And let us not grow weary while doing good, for in due season we shall reap if we do not lose heart.* As you sow your prayers in faith, I pray that you trust and believe God for your miracle, and don't let go until you receive.

Day 20 Get a Life

Read *The thief does not come except to steal, and to kill, and to destroy. I have come that they may have life, and that they may have **IT** more abundantly* (John 10:10).

What is the *it* that Jesus came for? Life. What is the *it* that the devil wants to steal from us? Life. It's all about life. But perhaps the question is whether we want to have life abundantly, or whether we are willing to let it be stolen from us.

Let's break this verse down a little further. The word "steal" comes from the word *klepto*, as in *kleptomaniac*. And what do kleptomaniacs do? They steal what does not belong to them. And isn't that a picture of the devil...stealing what doesn't belong to him...stealing what was intended for God's people? The word "kill" here means *to sacrifice or slaughter.* "Destroy" means *to put out of the way, abolish, put to an end, render useless, to give over to eternal misery of Hell, loss, and ruin.* Those are the things that the Bible says is part of the devil's strategy. He comes to destroy. And part of his purpose is to drag you along with him.

"...the question is whether we want to have life abundantly, or whether we are willing to let it be stolen from us."

It's so easy to just be consumed with the bad news when the good news might just be a sentence away. But praise God, there is more to this scripture, and it's important to keep reading. If we end on the first part of the sentence, we could miss the miraculous part—"I have come *so that...*" In other words, "I have come for the following purpose."

His purpose was and is *so that* we might have abundant life according to this scripture.

God sent His Son Jesus out of heaven, and I believe He did it for a good reason. His purpose in sending Jesus was so that you might have life and have it more abundantly. He did it so you could *have a life*—so you could *get a life*! And not just life as in survival, or life as in walking and breathing here on planet Earth. No, the word "life" in this verse actually means *all the highest and best that Christ is.*

I came so they can have real and eternal life, more and better life than they ever dreamed of.

—*John* 10:10 MSG

One way I've heard this scripture translated is that He came to exchange everything that we are for all the highest and best that He is—including His prosperity, increase, healing, health, wealth, wholeness, soundness, peace of mind—everything that He is. And He exchanged it for everything we are. He exchanged our weakness for His highest and best. What an amazing thing!

So, if we're carrying poverty, sickness, discouragement, or devastation, let's consider the reason Jesus came to Earth and see if by faith, in harmony with God's Word, there might be a need for a few exchanges in our life. Perhaps we could exchange our sorrow for His joy…our poverty for His prosperity as we sow into His kingdom and obey His Word… our sadness for His joy and gladness…and our sickness for the healing He purchased by the stripes on His back when He went to the cross (1 Peter 2:24).

"…the word abundant means the Lord has not only exchanged all that He is for all that we are, but He also gave us more than enough."

According to John 10:10, the word *abundant* means the Lord has not only exchanged all that He is for all that we are, but He also gave us more than enough. Not *just enough*. The word "abundant" means that He gave us *more than enough*— enough to spare, beyond measure, and superabundant in quantity. So, I believe that according to this one word, God intended for there to be more than enough for us, and still more than enough to share and to be a blessing to others. Now to me, that says something!

Pray Consider praying this prayer…
Lord, we thank You for coming to this earth to give us Your kind of life—the abundant, more-than-enough, God-kind of life that gives us hope and strengthens us to face every day with Your grace by faith. In the name of Jesus, we speak against any destruction, ruin, trouble, and robbery that the devil may be trying to attack us with, and we open our hearts to You and Your ways. In Jesus' name, amen.

Obey Consider this...

Now, if you haven't been living in the abundance that Jesus provided for you by His work on the cross, and you need to get a life—*His life*—then consider calling on Him to show you a plan—*His plan*—for your life. Consider spending time in His Word each day and let it guide you in making all your decisions, so that you can walk the path of abundant life that Jesus has for you.

And if you have never made a decision to accept Jesus into your heart, I encourage you to do it now. You can pray this simple prayer right now: *Heavenly Father, I make a decision to turn to You. I repent of my sins and I receive Your abundant life in every area of my life, according to what Jesus did on the cross for me. Thank You for giving me Your abundant life on earth and eternal life in heaven.*

And remember, you can call our Abundant Life® Prayer Group anytime, day or night, at 918-495-7777, and ask them to lead you to our abundantly merciful and loving Savior, the Lord Jesus Christ.

He who has the Son has life...

–1 John 5:12

Day 21 The Lukewarm Laodiceans

Read *I know your works, that you are neither cold nor hot. I could wish you were cold or hot. So then, because you are lukewarm, and neither cold nor hot, I will vomit you out of My mouth* (Revelation 3:15–16).

This passage of scripture in Revelation can give helpful insight to Christians. After reading it, we might think it was only meant for the church of Laodicea, but I believe it applies even more to Christians today. They certainly had troubles back then, but I sometimes wonder how many more things we struggle with today, because we have so much more media information to process and deal with.

So, let's go through this verse by verse, and let me ask questions along the way to see how this scripture might apply to our lives. In verses 15 and 16, Jesus says to us: *I know your works, that you are neither cold nor hot. I could wish you were cold or hot. So then, because you are lukewarm, and neither cold nor hot, I will vomit you out of My mouth.* I believe Jesus was saying, in a sense, that God wants us to be wholehearted Christians, not half-hearted...half the time living as the devil's crowd and half the time living a godly life. You see, God wants the best for His children. And living a lukewarm life is like straddling a fence. If you fall off, you'll get hurt. God has us in His hand to protect us and keep us from harm, and that's why He doesn't want us to get stuck in lukewarm thinking.

Years ago, in one of his amazing sermons, Oral explained it like this: "Lukewarmness is against God's Word. God said He hated it so much that He would vomit. Brother, when you get sick enough to vomit, you're sick! And that is what it seems that God is saying: 'I'm sick to my stomach.'" Oh my, that's something to think about, right?

And what is lukewarm? It is the mixing and mingling of hot and cold. Here, I think God is referring, on the one hand, to the things of God and what pleases Him, and on the other hand, the particular things of the world that are so far from His ways. The lukewarmness is a result of mixing and mingling these two ways of living. It's like having one foot serving the world and one foot serving God. While I realize we are in the world, the Bible clearly says we are *not of it* (John 15:19, John 17:15–16). If we are of God, then aren't we to be overcomers? We can keep in mind 1 John 4:4, which says, *Greater is He—Jesus—that is in us than he* [the devil] *who is in the world.* So, I believe we can live in the world and still please God by reflecting His nature, character, and way of life in Him.

"The luke-warmness is a result of mixing and mingling these two ways of living. It's like having one foot serving the world and one foot serving God."

I believe that as Christians, we're going to have to start being passionate about the things of God and the things He cares about, and not be so wrapped up and consumed with so many of the ungodly things of the world. Perhaps that's why God said, "Be hot or cold. Don't be lukewarm."

How do we make sure that we are on fire for the Lord so that He is pleased with us, and still live a balanced life on this earth? I believe God allows us to sow seed and give out of ourselves so we can be a blessing to others. The Bible tells us in Matthew 10:8 that because we have freely received, we ought to freely give. I believe we need to give of ourselves—our love, our time, our money, our talents—whatever God directs us to give. We can show others the way to eternal life, the way to the Father, which is by accepting Jesus Christ as Lord and Savior (John 14:6). As we give into what's important to God's heart, He can multiply that back in ways that are important to our heart (Luke 6:38).

Pray Consider praying this prayer...

Dear Heavenly Father, we thank You that You love us enough to correct, redirect, and forgive us when we miss the mark. And Lord, we declare a desire to please You and be more like You. Help us not to be lukewarm Christians, but rather help us to be totally committed to You. We repent for any times that we have been lukewarm in our faith, in our lives, and in our commitment to You. We receive the truth that You are faithful to forgive us and cleanse us from all unrighteousness, according to 1 John 1:9. In Jesus' name, amen.

Obey Consider this...

I encourage you to, as the Bible says, stir up your most holy faith (Jude 1:20) and look for ways to renew your passion for the things of the Lord. Begin to pray and sing songs of praise to Him. And most importantly, I encourage you to dig into His precious promises in the Bible to get a deeper revelation of what Jesus has done for you and who you are in Him!

But you, beloved, building yourselves up on your most holy faith, praying in the Holy Spirit, keep yourselves in the love of God, looking for the mercy of our Lord Jesus Christ unto eternal life.

—Jude 1:20–21

Day 22 The Spit, the Mud, and the Miracle

Read Now as Jesus passed by, He saw a man who was blind from birth. And His disciples asked Him, saying, "Rabbi, who sinned, this man or his parents, that he was born blind?" Jesus answered, "Neither this man nor his parents sinned, but that the works of God should be revealed in him. I must work the works of Him who sent Me while it is day; the night is coming when no one can work. As long as I am in the world, I am the light of the world." When He had said these things, He spat on the ground and made clay with the saliva; and He anointed the eyes of the blind man with the clay. And He said to him, "Go, wash in the pool of Siloam" (which is translated, Sent). So he went and washed, and came back seeing (John 9:1–7).

"When He combined the natural elements of the earth with the supernatural essence of God, the spit and the mud ignited into a miracle!"

Sometimes God uses the most unusual things to bring forth a miracle. Doesn't it seem strange that Jesus mixed together spit with mud to bring about a healing? But strange or not, He did! He did it to restore sight to a blind man. Jesus took the natural dirt of the earth and spit on it with the essence of His life—His DNA, so to speak. The Bible explains how this spiritual combination of the natural and the supernatural created an outflow of divine power. When He combined the natural elements of the earth with the supernatural essence of God, the spit and the mud ignited into a miracle!

In Genesis 2:7, the Bible says that we were created from the dust of the earth: *And the Lord God formed man of the dust of the ground, and breathed into his nostrils the breath of life; and* *man became a living being.* When God sent Jesus to Earth, He breathed His supernatural breath of life into Him. So, when Jesus spit on the dirt, wasn't He simply recreating sight in that blind man by using the elements God used in the first place? He took the dust of the earth that we were made from, added spit, which contained the essence of who He is, and the natural and supernatural joined together to create a healing miracle.

"... the natural and supernatural joined together to create a healing miracle."

And the Lord God formed man
of the dust of the ground, and breathed
into his nostrils the breath of life;
and man became a living being.

–Genesis 2:7

As we mix God's Word and the measure of faith that He has given to us (Romans 12:3), we can ask God to breathe His supernatural breath of life into it to make something miraculous.

According to Mark 11:22–24, the Bible says that we're to believe the Word of God by faith, in advance, or before the miracle happens. God has given us His Word so that we might know what He has to say and what He thinks about our situation until the manifestation of His power comes to us. Spiritually speaking, when you take the spit (the DNA, the essence of who Jesus is) and the mud (the dust we are created from, the essence of who we are) and infuse it with our faith, I believe that's when God can begin to intervene. I think that God wants us to see this as an example—almost like a parable—where Jesus told a natural story to explain a spiritual truth. I believe He was showing us how to join natural humanness with His divineness to expect a miracle.

Faith is a very important part of the equation. Hebrews 11 is a clear demonstration of people who allowed God to take the natural and mix it with the supernatural to bring about the miraculous. This passage of Scripture declares over and over again, "By faith, through faith, in faith." Four times the Scriptures boldly declare, *The just shall live by faith* (Habakkuk 2:4, Romans 1:17, Galatians 3:11, and Hebrews 10:38).

Hebrews 11:1 KJV says, *Now faith is the substance of things hoped for, the evidence of things not seen.* And God clearly stated in Romans 12:3 that He has given to us the measure of faith. To me, "the measure" means the measure you need to get the job done. Then He told us how to exercise and grow our faith in Romans 10:17 when He declared that faith comes by hearing the Word of God.

When Jesus healed the blind man, He mixed together what He had—God's Word and faith in God's power and willingness to heal. And just like Jesus, we can allow the infusion of the power of the Holy Spirit to mix with whatever we have that needs the touch of God. We can say, "Now faith is." Instead of just focusing on what the mess is in the natural, we can look to what God says and expect a miracle!

Pray Consider praying this prayer…

Father God, in the name of Jesus, we commit to do what we can in the natural, add the supernatural faith that You've already given us (Romans 12:3), and believe You can combine the two into a miracle in whatever situations we are facing. In the name of Jesus, we make a choice with our faith to expect a miracle. Amen.

Obey Consider this…

To me, one of the greatest of God's gifts and tools for our life is the gift of His Word and giving us the ability to declare it continuously. I encourage you to build a spiritual base, a foundation full of God's Word, by declaring it, believing it, and expecting it to come to pass according to Isaiah 55:11, which says that God's Word will not return back to us empty or void.

Now faith is the substance of things hoped for, the evidence of things not seen.

—Hebrews 11:1 KJV

Day 23 — Don't Be Deceived

Read *Jesus answered: "Watch out that no one deceives you"* (Matthew 24:4 NIV).

For false christs and false prophets will rise and show great signs and wonders to deceive, if possible, even the elect (Matthew 24:24).

Years ago, the Lord led me to do a Bible study on Jezebel, the evil queen who persecuted the prophet Elijah after he defeated the false priests of Baal on Mount Carmel. During my time of study, the Lord reminded me that one of the biggest tools of our enemy, the devil, is deception.

"If the devil can lure us away from the truth in God's Word, he can also lead us away from the safety within it."

I believe the devil uses deception as a way to draw us away from our relationship with God. If the devil can lure us away from the truth in God's Word, he can also lead us away from the safety within it. Remember, Psalm 91:1 tells us that when we abide—or remain—under the shadow of God's presence, we can enjoy the fullness of His protection. But if we leave that shadow (that protective covering where He becomes our refuge and our fortress), we can perhaps be an easier target for the devil's attacks against us.

So, what can we do? According to Matthew 24:4, we are to "watch out" so that we are not deceived. But it's up to us to learn how to recognize deception, so we can avoid it. In John 8:44, Jesus makes it clear that the devil is the source of all lies. Jesus, on the other hand, does not lie, and there is no deceit in Him (1 Peter 2:22). That leads me to believe that if we're going to be successful in avoiding deception, one thing we can do is to learn to separate God's truth from the lies of the enemy.

In John 14:6, Jesus declares, *"I am the way, the truth, and the life. No one comes to the Father except through Me."* And this statement sums up the difference between Jesus, whom the scriptures refer to as the Truth, and the devil, whom John 8:44 describes as the father of lies. Then John 10:10 tells us, *The thief* [devil] *does not come except to steal, and to kill, and to destroy. I* [Jesus] *have come that they may have life, and that they may have it more abundantly.* God's truth is to bring life to us, while the Bible says that the devil's lies can rob us and bring destruction.

He [Jesus] never sinned, nor ever deceived anyone.

–1 Peter 2:22 NLT

When we read about Elijah in 1 Kings 17–19, we can see that he faced several things that were trying to steal him away from his godly calling—things such as fear so strong that he felt the need to run away, discouragement that made his victory bitter, and self-doubt that made him feel abandoned by God. So, what led Elijah to deliverance? He heard what the Lord had to say to him about the situation, and it changed his attitude!

During our own times of trial, I believe we can use John 10:10 and examples from the lives of godly people like Elijah to learn how to be aware of the devil's attempts to lead us away from God's best for us. It's in knowing the truth of God's Word that we can begin to see the devil's lies for what they are. And when we do, we can then resist the enemy and believe he must flee from us, as James 4:7 says.

"The Holy Spirit has been sent to dwell within us as our Helper and guide in all things. So, we can turn to Him whenever we need that divine guidance."

And don't forget, we have the divine Helper, the Holy Spirit, who can guide us into God's truth. As Jesus said in John 16:13 KJV, *When he, the Spirit of truth, is come, he will guide you into all truth.* The Holy Spirit has been sent to dwell within us as our Helper and guide in all things. So, we can turn to Him whenever we need that divine guidance. He can help us whenever we need to discern what is true and what is false. We can call on Him to show us what is true as we read the Bible, as we pray, as we face the issues of life, as we make decisions about our future, and as we allow Him to guide us, He can lead us into all truth in all situations!

Pray Consider praying this prayer…
Father God, I commit today to put Your truth first in my life. Help me to see how I can avoid the enemy's deception in my life. I ask for insight into the truth found in Your Word and how I can apply it to my life, so that I can walk in Your light and Your truth every day. In Jesus' name, amen.

Obey

I believe that as Christians, we have a responsibility to the Lord to watch out for deception. We can strive to be like Jesus, in whom there was and is no deceit whatsoever. That may mean doing something simple, such as giving a little more time to reading God's Word—the truth—and making it a part of us, or we might want to ask the Lord to send His light and truth into areas that have been in darkness for us. Let's allow the Holy Spirit to show us what we can do today to embrace God's truth and avoid the devil's deceptions and lies, and then act on what He says.

Howbeit when he, the Spirit of truth, is come, he will guide you into all truth: for he shall not speak of himself; but whatsoever he shall hear, that shall he speak: and he will shew you things to come.

—John 16:13 KJV

Day 24 The Weapons of Our Warfare

Day 24

Read *For though we walk in the flesh, we do not war after the flesh: (for the weapons of our warfare are not carnal, but mighty through God to the pulling down of strong holds;) casting down imaginations, and every high thing that exalteth itself against the knowledge of God, and bringing into captivity every thought to the obedience of Christ* (2 Corinthians 10:3–5 KJV).

Many times in life, we can find ourselves dealing with situations in which our natural abilities seem limited, or our resources are not sufficient to rescue us. But we can serve a God who is unlimited! His Word says *His divine power has given to us all things that pertain to life and godliness* (2 Peter 1:3). And to me, one of the greatest things He has given us for success in this life is what Ephesians chapter 6 calls *the armor of God*. It's a spiritual armor that is designed to give us supernatural protection and spiritual weapons to help us stand strong in the face of what the Bible calls *the wiles of the devil*—the evil schemes that Satan uses to trip us up and push us off the course that God has set for our lives.

"The armor of God and the supernatural weapons of our warfare have God's divine power in them..."

While the devil may desire to show up at any time to try and tempt us, distract us, or trouble us (John 10:10), God has given us spiritual weapons, not based in our own limited natural abilities but in God's unlimited ability. The armor of God and the supernatural weapons of our warfare have

God's *divine power* in them—power to destroy the mistaken thoughts, the doubts, the fears, and other things that Satan uses against us. Those spiritual weapons are for us to use whenever we choose to use them. But God won't force us to use the weapons or wear His spiritual armor. It's up to us to be prepared and "battle-ready" at all times.

I preached a sermon once at Creflo and Taffi Dollar's World Changers Church International in Atlanta, Georgia, about the importance of being ready for battle on a daily basis. On the day of the service, I showed up with my hair a mess, no makeup on, and wearing a bathrobe. I'm sure I was a strange sight! I asked the congregation if I looked properly dressed and ready for the occasion, and of course they said no. But you see, that's what many of us do when difficult situations come. Sometimes we go into spiritual battle when we are not prepared or fully armored with the spiritual weapons we are given in Ephesians 6. We are not dressed for the occasion, so to speak.

To me, one of the most important things to know is that *whatever* the devil tries to do, God has given us His armor as protection. So, let's take a look at what God's armor can do for us, according to Ephesians 6:10–18.

First of all, God has provided us with the belt of truth, keeping in mind that Jesus is *the way, the truth, and the life* (John 14:6). When we know Jesus, we have access to God's Truth, rather than "truth" as seen through the eyes of human opinion or even the devil's deception. **Secondly,** we have the breastplate of righteousness. Righteousness means right-standing with God (the right way of doing things). **Third,** we have the shoes of peace. God gave us *His* shoes, the Gospel shoes of peace, so that when attacks come, we can stand strong in God's own peace (a word that means *nothing missing, nothing broken*)—a peace that passes all understanding and guards our mind from troubling thoughts and fears (Philippians 4:7).

Fourth, we have the shield of faith. The Bible says that God has already given each of us the measure of faith (Romans 12:3). So, we can shield ourselves against the devil and we can also build up our faith by hearing the Word of God (Romans 10:17). Remember, although we already have the amount, or the "measure," of faith we need, it's up to us to use it by praying, releasing our faith to God, sowing our seeds, speaking His Word, and expecting our miracle to come, because as Galatians 3:11 says, *the just shall live by faith.*

"As believers, we have every right to use God's Word as a spiritual weapon against the tricks and strategies of the devil."

Fifth, we have been given the helmet of salvation. In fact, salvation (the Greek word *sozo*) means *to save, keep safe and sound, to rescue from danger or destruction, to preserve, ensure salvation, heal, make whole.* The soldier's helmet guards his head against fatal injuries. Likewise, the devil may try to come against us by sending fear, worry, and doubt into our mind. But when we wear the helmet of salvation, protecting all God has given to us through the shed blood of Jesus, focusing on God's Word and His mercies to us, it can help us to resist the wrong ideas that the enemy would like to trap us into believing.

Sixth, we have the sword of the spirit, which is the Word of God. The Bible says God's Word is sharper than any two-edged sword (Hebrews 4:12). As believers, we have every right to use God's Word as a spiritual weapon against the tricks and strategies of the devil. That's why I put on the armor of God daily as a spiritual reminder of God's promises to me. In addition, Ephesians closes out with the instruction to "pray in the spirit." This reminds us to attach our faith in prayer when we "put on" God's armor.

Consider praying this prayer…

We thank You, Lord, for providing a powerful spiritual armor for us to use against the tricks and strategies of the devil. And as we put on the whole armor of God, we can stretch forth our faith believing to stand against any evil that may try to come against us. In Jesus' name, amen.

Obey Consider this…

Now that we know about the armor of the Lord, I believe we have to put it on. James 2:26 says, *Faith without works is dead.* And works mean corresponding action. So, as a spiritual action to represent our faith, we can take action by verbally acknowledging these pieces of armor when we get up every morning, or when we start our day. We can say in faith, *Heavenly Father, we acknowledge Your protective spiritual armor that You have provided for us. By faith, we put on the belt of truth, the breastplate of righteousness, the gospel shoes of peace, the shield of faith, the helmet of salvation, and the sword of the spirit, which is the Word of God.* And if challenges arise during the day, consider God's Word, the faith He has given to us, and what He said in Philippians 4:7: *And the peace of God, which surpasses all understanding, will guard your hearts and minds through Christ Jesus.*

And the peace of God, which surpasses all understanding, will guard your hearts and minds through Christ Jesus.

—Philippians 4:7

Day 25 By Faith

Read *Now faith is the substance of things hoped for, the evidence of things not seen… But without faith it is impossible to please Him, for he who comes to God must believe that He is, and that He is a rewarder of those who diligently seek Him* (Hebrews 11:1,6).

I was lying in bed one night studying my notes, getting ready to preach in a church the next morning, when the Lord spoke to my heart. He redirected me regarding the message I was going to preach. I felt God was telling me to minister about the critical importance of our faith.

I believe that to live in this day and age, as Christians, we have to live deeper in the Word. I believe that we have to take the Word of God to a higher level in our lives to overcome today's challenges, and that our faith must be active in order for us to walk in victory and success in this life. More and more every day, I see how important faith is. As Galatians 3:11 says, *The just shall live by faith*, and that faith has substance according to Hebrews 11:1, which says, *Now faith is the substance of things hoped for, the evidence of things not seen.* If we are facing times where things are "critical"—such as our health, our finances, our families, and so on—then I believe it is a critical time to have an understanding of the importance, the magnitude, and the power of our faith.

So, let's look again at Hebrews 11:1. Faith is a belief system that has substance. If we want to get God's answers, then shouldn't we be doing things God's way or according to His system of operating?

As I was studying, I read Hebrews 11:6, which says, *Without faith it is impossible to please Him.* So, in order to please God, we must be operating in His faith system—if there's no faith, there's no pleasing God. With faith, we *can* please Him; without it, we *can't.* That all made sense, and really, I was already familiar with this verse and its meaning.

"So, in order to please God, we must be operating in His faith system..."

But then the Lord led me to get a highlighter. At first, I thought it was the strangest thing I've ever heard! But what happened next was so amazing. I felt the strongest impression to highlight the word *faith* in each verse of Hebrews 11 KJV, beginning at verse 1, and going all the way down to verse 32. Then after I highlighted everything, the Lord told me to read just the highlighted parts aloud. Here is what it said:

Now faith, through faith, by faith Abel, by faith Enoch, but without faith, by faith Noah, by faith, by faith Abraham, by faith, through faith also Sara, these all died in faith, by faith Abraham, by faith Isaac, by faith Jacob, by faith Joseph, by faith Moses, by faith, by faith he forsook Egypt, through faith he kept the passover, by faith they passed through the Red sea, by faith the walls of Jericho fell down, by faith the harlot Rahab, who through faith, having obtained a good report through faith. And down to verse 32 which says, *And what more shall I say?*

I think I got the message! I got so excited because I was seeing in a whole new light just how critically important our faith is!

If we look very carefully at the way this chapter of Hebrews is presented, we usually see the people's faith before we even see who they are and what they experienced. I believe God did it that way on purpose because He wants us to understand that no matter what we've done, and no matter what is going on, or where we are headed, as we operate in faith and operate according to His Word, He can honor our faith.

So, how can we direct our faith? We can direct it to believe right or believe wrong, or we can choose to believe the truth or choose to believe a lie. We can choose to believe God's Word or choose to doubt it to pieces. We can choose to believe for the best or choose to fear the worst.

Then we can ask ourselves, "What do I have hidden in my heart—God's Word, or the doom and gloom of this world? Or both? Or maybe something in-between?" Psalm 119:11 says that we can hide God's Word in our heart. Matthew 12:34 says, *Out of the abundance of the heart the mouth speaks.* And Proverbs 18:21 KJV says, *Death and life are in the power of the tongue: and they that love it shall eat the fruit thereof.*

"...I believe that as we are squeezed by circumstances, God's Word can come up from our heart and out of our mouth, in faith. And then we can live by it..."

Now, if death and life are found in the power of the tongue, and they that love it shall eat the fruit of it, and if we hide God's Word in our heart, then I believe that as we are squeezed by circumstances, God's Word can come up from our heart and out of our mouth, in faith. And then we can live by it, as both the Old and New Testaments say, *The just shall live by faith* (Habakkuk 2:4, Romans 1:17, Galatians 3:11, and Hebrews 10:38).

Then to strengthen that God-given faith, we exercise Romans 10:17, which says that faith comes, or is developed or empowered, by hearing the Word of God. So to strengthen our faith, I see how crucial it is to get so filled with the Word of God that it can open the door for the miraculous.

Pray Consider praying this prayer…

*Heavenly Father, we thank You for Your Word, which represents Your will. As we read and study Your Word and act it out in faith, we ask You to watch over Your Word and bring it to pass, according to Jeremiah 1:12. Thank You, Lord, for giving us the **measure of faith** (Romans 12:3) and allowing us to live by it as we release it to You and honor Your Word. Help us to read, pray, and then obey Your Word, hide it in our hearts, and live an abundant life according to Your will. In Jesus' name, amen.*

Obey Consider this…

I encourage you to fill up your heart with the Word of God and allow Him to strengthen and *empower* your faith to see miracles in your life. Look up scriptures on faith and make a habit of studying them, and allow God to give you insight as to how they can apply to you.

So then faith comes by hearing, and hearing by the word of God.

—Romans 10:17

Ask the Little Boy

Read *He went through the country helping people and healing everyone who was beaten down by the Devil. He was able to do all this because God was with him* (Acts 10:38 MSG).

Have you ever heard anyone say, "Miracles aren't real," or "Miracles don't still happen today?" Well, people have said these kinds of things to me. When they do, my mind instantly goes back to an amazing story my father-in-law, Oral, liked to share. He called it, "Ask the little boy."

Many years ago, Oral was invited by Billy Graham to attend the World Congress on Evangelism in Berlin. While he was there, a minister from India approached him between sessions and asked, "Are you Oral Roberts? I've been wanting to meet you. One of the reasons I came was to meet you." Oral told him he was honored to hear that, and asked what he could do for him.

The man said, "I have a very difficult problem. I've never understood or believed in miracles or that God healed the sick, although I've preached for many years. Here is my problem. Two of my church members rushed into the service one day with their child who was dying. The doctors had just given up on him. The parents thrust their little child into my hands and said, 'Pastor, pray for God to heal him.' I was in a dilemma. They'd asked me to do what I didn't believe could happen—to ask God to heal. Before I realized it, though, I did pray for him, and to my utter amazement, God healed him."

Oral said, "What's the problem?" And the man said, "My problem is very serious. Did I do right? Did I do right in praying for the little boy?" Oral said he wanted to immediately reply, "Of course you did right! Of course you should have prayed for him. And God healed him. Give God thanks!" But the Holy Spirit stopped him. What came up from Oral's spirit was what I believe to have been a word of wisdom (1 Corinthians 12:8). He said to the man, "You want to ask me if you did right in praying for the little boy and God healed him?" The man said, "Yes." Oral's Holy Spirit-inspired response was: "Why don't you ask the little boy?"

"...I did pray for him, and to my utter amazement, God healed him."

Jesus said to him, "If you can believe, all things are possible to him who believes."

–Mark 9:23

The light bulb came on and the man suddenly understood. He exclaimed to Oral, "You have given me my answer, and I'm going back to India to have a healing ministry." Praise the Lord!

To me, as someone who has been sick and received a miracle from God, I had no question about the rightness of believing God for a miracle, or whether God still heals today. I am convinced we can spend hours, days, even weeks arguing whether or not miracles still happen today and get nowhere. But in my opinion, if we really want to know, we should consider finding someone who has experienced a miracle. We can ask them what they think, or better yet, ask God to personally allow us to experience His miracle healing power for ourselves. As Oral so often said, "A miracle settles the issue."

Oral also said, "One of the most important things in your life could just be a miracle, especially when you need one." In my experience, many people need God's miraculous power in their bodies, families, finances, and other areas. We need them ourselves, or someone we love needs one. The Bible tells us that His greatest wish for us is to prosper and be in health, even as our souls prosper (3 John 2). Praise God!

Pray Consider praying this prayer...
Father God, we thank You for Your Word in Acts 2:22 that tells us about miracles, signs, and wonders. Lord, as we release our faith, pray, and expect a miracle, we ask You for Your Word and Your will and Your power to be alive in us today. In Jesus' name, amen.

Obey Consider this...

Are you facing circumstances in your life today that just seem too big to conquer? Do you find yourself in a situation that seems too big for you to possibly escape? Well, the Bible says that when we believe according to God's will, nothing is impossible for those who believe (Mark 9:23). So, I encourage you to meditate on God's Word and consider saying, "Miracles belong in my day today." As you declare it, confess it and believe it, see what happens as a result of your faith in God's Word going into action.

"...the Bible says that when we believe according to God's will, nothing is impossible for those who believe."

God publicly endorsed Jesus the Nazarene by doing powerful miracles, wonders, and signs through him...

—Acts 2:22 NLT

The Prayer Cloth

Read *Now God worked unusual miracles by the hands of Paul, so that even handkerchiefs or aprons were brought from his body to the sick, and the diseases left them and the evil spirits went out of them* (Acts 19:11–12).

This scripture came to life in Richard and me when we were with his dad, Oral, as he was having a precautionary test done in the hospital. We had prayed over a prayer cloth and laid it on his bed. A nurse came in and removed it, but just then the doctor came in and said, "Oh, put that back! It contains their prayers." From then on, we saw the prayer cloth as a container of prayer, as a point of contact to release our faith.

Since the days of Acts 19, praying over handkerchiefs and other cloth items and laying them on the sick has been a Bible-honored method to pray for healing. Today, we call these items prayer cloths. For decades, Oral and Richard have been laying hands on prayer cloths and sending them all over the world as a point of contact for people in need of divine intervention, a miracle from the hand of God. I have carried a prayer cloth with me for many years. It is a reminder that I am covered in prayer, and it is a point of contact for me to stretch out my faith to God when I need a breakthrough in my life.

You may ask, "What is a point of contact?" The Bible teaches us in Romans 1:17 that the just shall live by their faith. Many times, Jesus said to people who came to Him for healing that it was their faith that made them whole. Hebrews 11:1 teaches us that *faith is the substance of things hoped for, the evidence of things not seen.* So to me, faith is a tangible, touchable substance that is, in a spiritual sense, what we hold on to as we pray. Our prayer has our belief system attached to it. Therefore, a point of contact provides a way for us to act on our belief, and when we do that, we release our faith to God. In a sense, a point of contact can be your connection to Him as you set the time and place for your agreement with His Word.

Now faith is the substance of things hoped for, the evidence of things not seen.

—Hebrews 11:1

A point of contact may be many different things. Our point of contact could be the prayer of faith…the laying on of hands…the Holy Communion…a prayer cloth. Ultimately, a point of contact is simply the method we use to reach out to God to connect in prayer and to agree with His Word and His will for our life.

In the Bible, people approached God in many different ways, but each of them in their own way used what I see as a point of contact to release their faith to Him. The woman with the issue of blood touched the hem of Christ's

"…a point of contact is simply the method we use to reach out to God to connect in prayer and to agree with His Word and His will for our life."

garment. The laying on of hands of Christ and the apostles, the wearing of handkerchiefs and aprons (prayer cloths) from Paul's body, the shadow of Peter, the staff of Moses, the mantle of Elijah—all demonstrate something people could attach their faith to, and then release their faith and point it directly to God in prayer.

The point of contact is such a simple truth. I believe that because the use of prayer cloths is recorded in the Bible, God intends for us to connect with it and that it wasn't just for Bible days; I believe it is for every day.

Pray Consider praying this prayer...
Heavenly Father, we thank You for showing us that we have a Bible right to stretch out our faith for miracles. And Lord, we thank You that Your Word says You want us blessed in every area of our lives—spirit, soul, and body; faith, family, and finances—as we stretch out our faith to You. Thank You for Your saving, healing, delivering power that is available to me. In Jesus' name, amen.

Obey

Consider this...

I encourage you to read Acts 19 to learn more about the Apostle Paul and the handkerchiefs and aprons that were used as a point of contact to bring God's healing power to the sick. Allow the Holy Spirit to build your faith so that you can apply this biblical principle in your own life. If you would like to request a prayer cloth for you or your loved one, you can call the Abundant Life® Prayer Group at 918-495-7777, or go online at www.oralroberts.com/bookstore.

The just shall live by faith.

—Romans 1:17

Blessed to Be a Blessing

Read *Praise ye the Lord. Blessed is the man that feareth the Lord, that delighteth greatly in his commandments. His seed shall be mighty upon earth: the generation of the upright shall be blessed. Wealth and riches shall be in his house: and his righteousness endureth for ever* (Psalm 112:1–3 KJV).

The meaning of this scripture seems to jump off the page in the *Message* version of the Bible, as it says, *Blessed man, blessed woman, who fear God, who cherish and relish his commandments.* I love that expression—cherish and relish his commandments.

"If I'm blessed, then my children, my family, and my home can have an opportunity to be blessed also."

Verses 2 and 3 tell us that our seed—meaning our children—can be mighty on the earth. Our generation, or family, can be blessed, and we can have wealth and riches in our house. If I'm blessed, then my children, my family, and my home can have an opportunity to be blessed also.

But why is it so important that we have this blessing? I don't think God is against wealth and riches, or else why would He say, *Wealth and riches shall be in his house* (Psalm 112:3)? According to Proverbs 13:22, a good man leaves an inheritance for his children and his children's children. It takes resources or "something" to leave an inheritance for two generations. But while I'm all for leaving an inheritance to my children, let's look at a few other scriptures to see the blessing in it. The Bible not only speaks of an inheritance for our children; it also speaks of blessing our children. We can trace the concept of blessing back to Abraham, who was both a godly man and also one of great wealth (Genesis 13:2 and Genesis 24:1). So, the Bible tells us that we are to have an inheritance and blessings, but does it give us insight as to how to use them?

Let them shout for joy and be glad, who favor my righteous cause; and let them say continually, "Let the Lord be magnified, Who has pleasure in the prosperity of His servant."

—Psalm 35:27

Well, Genesis 12:2 says, *I will bless you and make your name great; and you shall be a blessing.* This tells us that it's not just about having a blessing, but it's also about being a blessing. Therefore, I believe one reason for this blessing is to touch others with the love of Jesus Christ and to share the heart of our Father God with them. I believe the blessings of God are designed to supply our need *according to His riches in glory by Christ Jesus* (Philippians 4:19) and also to give us the heart and the substance to reach out to others.

The Word of God says in Psalm 35:27 that the Lord delights in the prosperity of His people. He gives us power to get wealth, according to Deuteronomy 8:18. He gave man dominion, or control, over the earth and the riches in it (Genesis 1:26). This is not man's opinion, but God's Word. He decides how to honor His Word and bless His people. Malachi 3:10–11 says that we are to bring tithes and offerings into the storehouse (God's house), and when we do, God opens the windows of heaven, pours us out a blessing, and rebukes the devourer for our sake. Luke 6:38 says that when we give, God multiplies it back to us good measure, pressed down, shaken together, and running over. Philippians 4:19 says we have a heavenly account and when we sow, we have a Bible right to watch God supply all our needs according to His riches in glory.

So, why does the Bible say all this? For what reason? Well, according to these scriptures, God not only wants us to be blessed personally, but to have the resources to be a blessing to others. I believe that our prosperity is an opportunity to be a blessing by reaching out to others, and that's what I call a win-win situation.

Pray Consider praying this prayer…
Father, we thank You that Your Word says You want us to be blessed in every area of our lives. As we sow our seed "as unto the Lord" in obedience to Your Word, we trust You to supply more than enough to us and then for us to bless others as You instruct. In Jesus' name, amen!

Obey

Consider this...

Good intentions sound good in theory, but as James 2:17 says, faith without works is as good as dead. Works here represent corresponding action. So, consider stretching out your faith with corresponding seed/action planted unto God, and then expect a miracle harvest according to His Word in Luke 6:38 and Galatians 6:7.

Wealth and riches will be in his house, and his righteousness endures forever.

—Psalm 112:3

Day 29 Oh My Word!

Read For assuredly, I say to you, whoever says to this mountain, "Be removed and be cast into the sea," and does not doubt in his heart, but believes that those things he says will be done, he will have whatever he says. Therefore I say to you, whatever things you ask when you pray, believe that you receive them, and you will have them (Mark 11:23–24).

To me, this verse is one of the foundational scriptures of faith. It is like bedrock, spiritually speaking. But there is one small word in this scripture that makes a very big difference—and that is the word *say*.

What we say can make an enormous difference in the outcome of a situation. So, let's look at a few scriptures that explain the spiritual power that our words can have. Proverbs 18:21 says, *Death and life are in the power of the tongue, and those who love it will eat its fruit.* The life and death of a situation, spiritually speaking, can be found in the power of words. According to this scripture, we can potentially have a game-changer through the power of the words in our mouth.

Our words are formed by the tiny part of our body known as the tongue. James 3:4–5 says, *Look also at ships: although they are so large and are driven by fierce winds, they are turned by a very small rudder wherever the pilot desires. Even so the tongue is a little member and boasts great things. See how great a forest a little fire kindles!* Even though the tongue is relatively small, it can have a big impact on our lives.

So, the way I see it, one of the most important reasons to be careful of what we say is that we are sowing seeds through the words of our mouths, and we can expect those seeds to take root and bring a harvest, whether it be a good harvest or a bad one. So if that's true, then according to the Bible, I believe we have to be aware of our words in every situation.

With all that is going on in the world today, I have become even more diligent about my words. I hear people say, "I'm afraid of this or that" in a very casual manner, but the Bible says, *Do not fear* (Luke 12:32). So I try to line up my words with His Words, stay in faith, and say, "I will not fear!" When our words agree with God's Word, I believe we open the door for Him to bring His promises to pass in our lives. And am I perfect about this? No. But I try to make it a positive thing about awareness rather than a negative thing about perfection.

Over and over, I hear people say things like, "Wait until you hear this; it will just kill you," or "It's so amazing I could just die," or "It's to die for." Really? Is it? I realize this may sound picky, but the Bible says we will give an account of every idle word we speak (Matthew 12:36). And again, it's not about being perfect. It's more about closing the door on the devil so he has no opportunity to use our words against us.

"...we will give an account of every idle word we speak (Matthew 12:36)."

The Bible says that we are to watch our words and speak them with power. The Bible also says that we can be snared by the very words of our mouth (Proverbs 6:2). So, I don't want to open the door to the devil with disregard for my words or the power behind them. Since we have accountability for the many words we speak each day, I sincerely try to choose them carefully with meaning and purpose. Yes, of course, I chat and have the normal conversations of life with my friends and family. But when it comes to opening the door to the devil with my words, I have genuinely made a specific choice to watch my words and give the devil no place (Ephesians 4:27). And if I'm "spending" my words today, perhaps they can be better "spent" by declaring God's Word, in faith, over the situation I'm facing in order to attract the saving, healing, delivering power of God.

"...use God's Words. His Words already have His anointing on them. His Words are designed to bring His will to pass."

You may ask, "What if I don't know what to say?" I believe the answer is quite clear according to the Bible—use God's Words. His Words already have His anointing on them. His Words are designed to bring His will to pass. So to me, it's very important for us to draw on His power and anointing as we speak over our lives and pray in faith. As we do, I believe we can see His power—*"For My thoughts are not your thoughts, nor are your ways My ways," says the Lord... "So shall My word be that goes forth from My mouth; it shall not return to Me void, but it shall accomplish what I please, and it shall prosper in the thing for which I sent it"* (Isaiah 55:8,11).

I have given a lot of scriptures today, but my message comes down to two things that I believe can help set us up for success when it comes to our words. **First,** we can watch our words—our tongue can be a destructive weapon or a soothing balm. **Second,** we can pray His Word—God's anointing is already on His Words, so as we use them in faith, we can expect His results.

Pray Consider praying this prayer…

Lord, we pray now in the name of Jesus and ask that You would help us continually guard our words and the thoughts of our hearts so that they are pleasing to You. As we line up our words with Your Word—the Bible—we choose to speak faith into our circumstances. In Jesus' name, amen.

Obey Consider this…

As a gentle reminder, I want to encourage you to do as Romans 12:2 says: *Do not be conformed to this world, but be transformed by the renewing of your mind, that you may prove what is that good and acceptable and perfect will of God.* We can evaluate what we are putting into our minds on a daily basis. I encourage you to surround yourself with good news and add something positive to your life daily from the Word of God. And remember, our prayer partners at the Abundant Life® Prayer Group would be glad to pray with you anytime, day or night, at 918-495-7777.

And I tell you this, you must give an account on judgment day for every idle word you speak.

–Matthew 12:36 NLT

Day 30 — For God So Loved

> *Read* For God so loved the world, that he gave his only begotten Son, that whosoever believeth in him should not perish, but have everlasting life (John 3:16 KJV).

Have you ever thought about why it is so important to God that people should not perish? In his Bible commentary, Oral talks about the fact that God had lost His children when Satan tempted them and they had to leave the Garden of Eden. God's masterpiece, His creation, His children made in His image, had been stolen through the temptation of Satan (Genesis 3).

"God felt a deep need to get His children back, even if it meant giving His only begotten Son as a ransom for His stolen children."

According to the Bible, God felt a deep need to get His children back, even if it meant giving His only begotten Son as a ransom for His stolen children. So Jesus went to the cross to conquer our sin and redeem us to the Father.

But why did Jesus do this? Why did He plant this remarkable seed? He did it for a purpose! Oral explains that this gives us a beautiful picture of seed-faith. **First,** God had a need—to redeem His lost creation. **Second,** God so loved that He gave. He made His love an act of giving. Oral used to say you can give without loving, but you can't love without giving. **Third,** God gave His best, and He called it a seed. And **fourth,** God gave to receive. He gave for a desired result—you and me!

According to the Bible, the restoration of God's children was the greatest harvest of all. God's seed-planting went into action when Jesus went to the cross for our sins. He was given so that we, God's children, could have the gift of salvation and eternal life with Him. Now as John 3:16 says, we do not have to perish; we can have everlasting life by believing in Jesus.

Behold what manner of love the Father has bestowed on us, that we should be called children of God!

–1 John 3:1

So, it's not just what God did for us, but why He did it. It's the two simple words, "so loved." Two words—seven letters—but it's a powerhouse of meaning to me. God's love is everlasting, all encompassing, totally unconditional, and almost unexplainable. It knows no end and has no limits. His love is so unusual that it is not there to smother, but to cover...not to squeeze the life out of you, but to place His life within you. The Bible says that every good and perfect gift comes from God (James 1:17) and that He knows the plans He has for You (Jeremiah 29:11). They are plans for your good and not for evil.

Our family has an acquaintance who has written a song about the love of God. Basically, the only words in it simply reference God's love. One evening we were visiting some-one's home, and this songwriter sat at the piano next to my husband, and they began to sing about the love of God. Immediately I began weeping. I was embarrassed to look up, wondering what the roomful of people would think of me. As I looked up, I noticed every person in the room was experiencing the same emotion as I was. When they began to sing about the love of God in this beautifully anointed song, the meaning of God's love seemed to overtake us.

"I know that, as a parent, I want the best for my children... How much more must God truly love us?"

It's amazing to me that when we truly comprehend the love of God, it's almost unexplainable. It's impossible to put into words. I know that, as a parent, I want the best for my children. There are almost no words to explain my love for them. How much more must God truly love us? And while Satan, the devil, wants to separate us from God and His love, I believe that when we really know the love of God, it's like a magnet that draws us and keeps us close to Jesus.

Pray Consider praying this prayer...
Father God, we are thankful today that You loved us so much that You gave. And You didn't give half-heartedly. You gave Your very best—Your only begotten Son. When needs arise in our lives, we commit to try to give our best each time, believing that what we give is what You can multiply back. We believe our good seed will bring a good harvest. Thank You for showing us opportunities to be a blessing to people, and to show them the love of God. Teach us how to sow for a desired result, according to Your Word, and then expect a miracle that only You can bring to pass. In Jesus' name, amen.

Obey Consider this…

I encourage you now to make a conscious effort to expect a miracle every day. My mother-in-law, Evelyn, used to hear the phone ring and then say, "Lord, is this my miracle?" As she opened her mail, she would say, "Is this my miracle?" She lived in a constant state of expecting God's miracles in her life. So I encourage you to be aware of giving to God, releasing your faith, and expecting a new miracle every day.

By this we know love,
because He laid
down His life for us.

—1 John 3:16

He Was Dying to Meet You

Day 31

Read ...*faith without works is dead* (James 2:26).

At the risk of repeating myself, I want to demonstrate something to you that takes the devotional from Day 30, "For God So Loved," and shows you here in Day 31 the "action" of God. As James 2:26 says, *faith without works is dead.* When we look at that scripture carefully, we recognize that part of acting in faith is the word *works*, which means *corresponding actions.* When we act in faith, a corresponding action must follow, or that faith can begin to "die on the vine," so to speak. So, what is the corresponding action of recognizing the love of God?

For God loved us so much, He did something about it! He went into action. And what was that action? He sent His Son, Jesus, to leave heaven and all of its glory (walls made out of jasper, gates made out of pearl, streets made out of gold, no sin or sorrow, no suffering, and so on) to come to Earth because of God's great love for humankind.

God sent Jesus into the world through a young girl named Mary so that as the Son of God, He knew God's divineness, and as the son of human flesh, He knew the life of humankind. My father-in-law, Oral, used to say that Jesus was so much God, it was as if He was not a man, yet He was so much man, it was as if He was not divine. Jesus genuinely knew both worlds—the world of the Spirit of God and the world of the flesh, or humanity. But because God loved us so much, He allowed His Son not just to be born, but to

> "For God loved us so much, He did something about it! He went into action. And what was that action? He sent His Son, Jesus..."

show us, in the flesh, how God intended us to live—healed and whole, prosperous and delivered.

But for all of humanity's sins, God sent His Son to pay the final price, the extreme sacrifice—the cross. The Bible says with the stripes on His back and His shed blood on the cross, He forever paid the price for the redemption of mankind (Ephesians 2:13, 1 John 1:7). He reunited God and humankind through the cross.

Sometimes God uses life experiences to get a message like this across to us. That's what happened to me one day in the grocery store. A woman came running toward me, her arms waving, as she hollered, "Lindsay, it's really you! I was just dying to meet you!" This lady was so sincere, and I was humbled by her desire to meet me. But God used that encounter to speak to my heart. I felt His words deep in my soul: "No, *I* was dying to meet you at the very point of your needs."

I began to think about those words and Jesus' sacrifice for me. I thought about the crucifixion of my Lord—the 39 stripes He took on His back for our healing, the walk down the Via Dolorosa (the Way of Suffering), and the trip up the hill of Golgotha, the Place of the Skull. There on the cross, the sinless, blameless Son of the Living God died for our sins. Isaiah 53:5 says, *He* [Jesus] *was wounded for our transgressions; He was bruised for our iniquities.* And Isaiah 52:14 NIV says, *His appearance was so disfigured beyond that of any man and his form marred beyond human likeness.* It was suffering beyond our comprehension.

The amazing thing to me is that when Jesus hung on the cross, He had you and me on His mind and in His heart. We were the reason He was there, and He was willing to pay the price to redeem us. And that's the love that Jesus has for us! The Bible says *God is love* (1 John 4:8). It doesn't say He *has* love; it says He *is* love. God loves us all the time—every minute of every day—unconditionally.

And although nothing can separate us from God's amazing love, unrepented sin—which is sin we have not asked God to forgive us for—can keep us from eternal life. Romans 6:23 KJV says, *For the wages of sin is death; but the gift of God is eternal life through Jesus Christ our Lord.* And although God loves us as we are, He loves us enough to want us to change our sinful lives so we can have eternal life with Him in heaven.

Too often we think we have to get "all cleaned up" to come to the Lord and receive His love, but that's not true. It's not about becoming "good enough" in our own humanness to earn salvation. Salvation comes to each of us by God's gift of grace. Ephesians 2:8 says, *For by grace you have been saved through faith, and that not of yourselves; it is the gift of God.*

It's not about what we've done or how far down we are. The Bible says that if we will turn to God and call out to Him, He hears us and receives us. God sent His only Son to purchase our salvation. We are God's prize—His treasure. He has paid no higher price for anything than He paid for us.

As God put His love into action for you and me, if we choose to turn to God, the Bible says it requires an action. Sadly, many people believe the required action is perfection—to get perfect before we come to God—but that's not what the Bible says. The action God requires is found in Romans 10:9–10, which simply says, *If you confess with your mouth the Lord Jesus and believe in your heart that God has raised Him from the dead, you will be saved.* In Romans 10:13 He says, *Whoever calls on the name of the Lord shall be saved.*

So, the corresponding action required is to call upon the name of the Lord, repent of our sins, and simply receive our salvation by faith. Remember, Ephesians 2:8 says, *For by grace you have been saved through faith, and that not of yourselves; it is the gift of God.* As Jesus laid down His life as the greatest gift we could receive, if you have not already done so, I encourage you to consider praying the sinner's prayer to receive that gift of salvation.

Pray Consider praying this prayer…

Father God, I thank You for Your mercy to me, even though I was a sinner, a backslider, or simply did not know You. I repent of every wrongdoing. I ask You to forgive me and cleanse me. And now, by faith, I receive Jesus Christ, God's only Son, as my Lord and Savior. I believe You have made a place for me in heaven to live an eternal, abundant life with You. I declare that I am born again. I'm a new person, a child of God. In Jesus' name, amen.

Obey Consider this…

I believe that because of God's amazing love, He was dying to meet you at the point of your need, and because of God's miraculous resurrection power, He lives forevermore and invites you to live with Him eternally and call heaven your ultimate home. And because of what Jesus did on the cross, you have the Bible right—as a child of God—to accept *all* that He has done for you. If you are living anywhere away from God's highest and best for you, I encourage you to study the Bible, the Word of God, and find out all God has for you. I truly believe He wants to heal your body, your relationships, your family, your finances, your emotions—any and every need you have. I encourage you to begin to expect a miracle and declare it by faith and receive it according to God's perfect will for your life.

Lindsay Roberts is co-host of *The Place for Miracles*, a powerful daily interactive healing program, where she joins her husband, Richard, in preaching and praying for the needs of viewers. In addition, she hosts the inspirational women's television program, *Make Your Day Count*. Lindsay also serves as editor of *Miracles* and *Make Your Day Count* online magazines for Oral Roberts Ministries. She is the author and co-author of several books, including *36 Hours with an Angel*, *Overcoming Stress*, and a series of devotionals for women, mothers, teachers, and teens. She ministers at women's conferences and other services around the country.

ABUNDANT
LIFE
PRAYER GROUP

For prayer anytime,
call **918-495-7777**,
or log on to our website at
www.oralroberts.com/prayer.